'His suitably monumental work . . . For the scientifically challenged, one of the great virtues of Brindle's book is its charitable explanations of the intricacies of engineering . . . The book also goes some way to unpick the character of Brunel . . . in carefully selected oils and prints, there are numerous glimpses of the public responses to his work . . . this book provides a superb commentary on Brunel's industriousness, vision, and technical brilliance. He might not have been the greatest Briton, but after reading this wonderful work all should concur that Brunel can lay claim to the title of Britain's greatest engineer'   Tristram Hunt, *History Today*

'The content is detailed, but nonetheless entertaining for anyone simply requiring an enjoyable book . . . It gives an intriguing insight into the character of a great engineer, pursuing sometimes too ambitious ideas and plans'
                     Bill Richmond, *Times Educational Supplement*

'It's to Steven Brindle's credit that he lets Britain's greatest engineer speak for himself here'   *BBC Focus*

'A jewel of a book, enthusiastically introduced by the estimable Cruickshank . . . Readers will be entranced by the saga of Sir Marc Brunel (1769–1849 – the French-born builder of the first tunnel under the Thames) and his son . . . The author tells brilliantly the amazing adventure of the imagining, the construction, and the launch of *Leviathan*, a giant ship that ruined its backers but eventually laid the first successful transatlantic cable. This is more than a scintillating portrait of a genius, it's a fascinating and edifying picture of Britain surging to leadership and prosperity in a hopeful and glorious age'   *Good Book Guide*

Steven Brindle is a highly respected author and historian. He read History at Keble College, Oxford and currently works for English Heritage as Inspector of Ancient Monuments for Greater London. He is a leading authority on Brunel and is famed for discovering and saving Brunel's 'lost' iron bridge at Paddington in 2003. His previous books include the critically acclaimed *Paddington Station: Its History and Architecture*.

Dan Cruickshank is a regular BBC presenter, best known for his popular series 'Around the World in 80 Treasures' and 'Britain's Best Buildings'. He is a leading expert in architecture and historic buildings and he is an active member of the Georgian Group and the Architectural Panel of the National Trust. His previous books include the bestselling *Around the World in 80 Treasures*, and *Life in the Georgian City*.

Brunel

THE MAN WHO BUILT THE WORLD

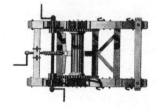
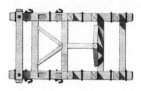

STEVEN BRINDLE

with an Introduction by
Dan Cruickshank

WEIDENFELD & NICOLSON

A W&N PAPERBACK

First published in Great Britain in 2005
by Weidenfeld & Nicolson
This paperback edition published in 2006
by Weidenfeld & Nicolson,
an imprint of Orion Books Ltd,
Carmelite House, 50 Victoria Embankment,
London EC4Y 0DZ

An Hachette UK Company

14

Introduction © Dan Cruickshank
Text © Steven Brindle
Original design and layout copyright
© Weidenfeld & Nicolson 2005

Edited by Matt Lowing
Original hardback design by Ken Wilson
Picture research by Brónagh Woods
Editorial by Ilsa Yardley, David Atkinson and Slav Todorov
Index by Chris Bell
Additional photography by David Jones

A CIP catalogue record for this book
is available from the British Library.

ISBN 978-0-7538-2125-1

Printed and bound by
CPI Group (UK) Ltd, Croydon, CR0 4YY

The Orion Publishing Group's policy is to use papers
that are natural, renewable and recyclable products and
made from wood grown in sustainable forests. The logging
and manufacturing processes are expected to conform to
the environmental regulations of the country of origin.

www.orionbooks.co.uk

Acknowledgements

The authors wish to thank and acknowledge the many people who have generously given of their time and knowledge during the writing and production of this book. Lawrence Hurst, Derek Sugden and Malcolm Tucker gave much invaluable advice on engineering matters; Thomas Berne and John Berne provided insights into Brunel's final illness; Julia Elton, Simon Kirsop, James Sutherland and Liz Whitbourn provided much helpful advice and comment. The staff of Bristol University Library's Special Collections, the British Library, English Heritage's library, the National Archives and Westminster Archives were unfailingly efficient and helpful. We would like to thank Mr Stephen Hurst, the staff of the Bridgeman Art Library, the Hulton Getty Picture Collection, the National Railway Museum, STEAM – Museum of the Great Western Railway in Swindon and the Science Museum, for all their help in assembling the illustrations for this book. Our special thanks go to Charles Walker, the designer Ken Wilson and to Michael Dover, Matt Lowing and Brónagh Woods at Weidenfeld & Nicolson for all of their efforts in making this book a reality.

Contents

Introduction

Isambard Kingdom Brunel remains one of the most inspiring and compelling figures of the 19th century. A man born into the old world yet pivotal in the creation of the modern age, Brunel appears the very quintessence of the inventive, creative and pioneering spirit of Victorian Britain. When Brunel was born in 1806 Britain had just won a great naval victory over France – the native country of Brunel's father – and the triumphant fleet was composed of ships built of oak, powered by wind and essentially little changed from warships of 300 years earlier. The man-made world that the young Brunel inhabited was wrought of brick, timber or stone and most goods and people travelled across the land using horse power. By the time Brunel died in 1859 all this had changed – iron-hulled and steam-powered ships had arrived, pioneering new materials and methods of construction had been utilised in the fabrication of buildings that – in their scale and design – were like nothing man had ever constructed before and the road and the canal were being challenged by the new railway system with horse power gradually being replaced by steam power. These radical developments had their origins in the second half of the 18th century in what is now termed the Industrial Revolution, but most came to fruition and started to change the look and life of Britain during the few decades between 1825 and 1855 – and many of the most dramatic changes were due directly to Brunel's inventive energy and leaping imagination.

It is now fascinating to reconstruct the world of the young Brunel – and vital to do so – for only by placing him in the context of his times is it possible to begin to understand him and to realise fully the scale of his achievement. In August 1822, at the age of 16, he returned to London from France to start working in the office of his father, the engineer and inventor Marc Brunel. Marc had just undergone a trauma that seems to come right out of the pages of Dickens. Like William Dorrit in *Little Dorrit* and, indeed, like Dickens' own father, Marc had been imprisoned for debt, not in the Marshalsea but in King's Bench Prison in Southwark, following the collapse or miscarriage of various business enterprises. In fact Dickens' early novels provide a framework for the reconstruction of young Brunel's early life in London. He and Dickens were near contemporaries in age, both born in or near Portsmouth, and the world Dickens evoked in the *Pickwick Papers*, published in 1836, is the world Brunel would have known. Pickwick dined in the George and Vulture off Cornhill, a few hundred yards from the office in Poultry where Marc – a free man once again in 1822 – had not only re-established himself in business but was on the threshold of the most ambitious engineering project of his career. In 1823 Marc was appointed engineer for the burrowing of the Thames Tunnel between Wapping and Rotherhithe – an heroic undertaking that would serve as young Brunel's introduction to the alarming, and occasionally downright dangerous, realities of pioneering civil engineering.

The world the young Brunel knew, that formed his character, was the world of late Georgian Britain, of the Regency, and despite being one of the pioneers of the modern world, Brunel remained in many of his tastes, beliefs and attitudes a Regency buck until his dying day. He liked style in all things – certainly in his clothes; he loved the arts, picturesque landscape and eclectically ornamental architecture. He was class conscious, decidedly authoritarian with those he considered his social inferiors, supported conservative social values – Brunel served as a special constable in Bristol during the riots of 1831 provoked by the slow passage of the Reform Bill and in Westminster in 1848 during the Chartist protests – believed in gentlemanlike conduct in all his dealings, and cherished the status of being an English gentleman and readily accepted the obligations that went with it. So Brunel, although a most modern man in his professional life, lived by an old-fashioned, somewhat snobbish but high-principled code of honour. Unlike the modern businessman, profit and commercial success were not all for Brunel. He held an all-embracing vision for the modern world – giving mankind the benefits latent in the inspired application of new technology but without abandoning traditional and honourable values. He wanted to satisfy his clients, meet their practical demands and give them the expected return on their investments – but not at any price. Brunel also served a higher master – he was a romantic idealist driven to visionary heights in his quest for excellence, in his burning ambition to attain what, in earlier ages, had appeared to be merely impossible dreams.

The teenage Brunel, walking through the City to his father's office at 26 Poultry or from the Georgian house at 30 Bridge Street, Blackfriars, into which Marc Brunel moved his staff and family in June 1824, to the engineering works of Maudslay, Son & Field in Lambeth, was treading a strange and uncharted path. In the City Brunel would have passed the great engineering works of the 17th and 18th centuries, from Robert Mylne's spectacular stone-built and Piranesian Blackfriars Bridge, completed in 1769, below the great

structural wonder of late 17th-century London, Wren's St
Paul's dome, and through the maze of City alleys and courts,
still medieval in feel. And in Lambeth he would have been in
London's industrial quarter – among mills, engineering
works, manufactories and wharfs. These areas would have
been heaving with life, enterprise and energy – but all was
soon to change. Brunel was walking between two worlds and
he carried the future with him. What could he have thought,
what could he have imagined as he surveyed the scene he
walked through? Within a few years vast swathes of the
traditional city were to be swept away by the great railway
companies – a traumatic experience for Londoners as
expressed in most vivid manner by Dickens in the mid-1840s
in *Dombey and Son* where he describes the demolitions and
earthworks associated with the construction of Euston
Station and its approaches by the London & Birmingham
Railway. It was, wrote Dickens, as if 'a great earthquake had,
just at that period, rent the whole neighbourhood into its
centre . . . houses were knocked down; streets broken
through and stopped; deep pits and trenches dug in the
ground, enormous heaps of earth and clay thrown up;
buildings that were undermined and shaking, propped by
great beams of wood . . . Everywhere were bridges that led
nowhere, thoroughfares that were wholly impassable; Babel
towers of chimneys . . . and giant forms of cranes, and
tripods straddling above nothing . . . In short, the yet
unfinished and unopened Railroad was in progress.'

Such, in cities at least, was the physical consequence of
the vision of Brunel and his fellow railway engineers and
investors. And much that survived such a direct physical
assault was to be challenged or compromised by the works of
this new breed of men. The coaching inns – venerable
institutions which Dickens evokes with great nostalgia in

Pickwick – were to give way to the railway station, while river and canal trade and the Thames-side wharfs were gradually to bow to the rail system. Within this traditional and seemingly timeless world walked and toiled the young Brunel, the man who was to prove, in his works if not his attitudes, the great agent of change, a one-man industrial revolution.

So Brunel is a paradox – rooted in the old world he imagines, and helps create, the new. As an engineer he is a man who has to contend with objective facts, with the possibilities and potentials of materials and means of construction, a man who has to be able to calculate all he sees and proposes. Yet Brunel is also an out-and-out romantic. This is revealed by all he does – in the home he created from 1836 for his family in the rooms above his office in Duke Street, Westminster, where he embellished his neo-Gothic dining room with specially commissioned paintings showing scenes from Shakespeare, in his proposals for his country estate in Devon and – above all – in the architecture he envisioned and realised for the Great Western Railway. In his engineering works Brunel was ruthless and clinical in his methods as he moved to ever more minimalist and utilitarian structures stripped of the conventions of ornament – culminating with the mighty Saltash Bridge that was completed in the year of his death. But in his art Brunel was quite another man, extravagant and wayward – the archetypal romantic, almost unrealistic, artist who believed in big and bold gestures that could not be measured in monetary terms.

The Great Western Railway was among the first great railway systems in the world, pioneering many aspects of railway design. The offices and station at Temple Meads formed the world's first functionally and architecturally coherent railway terminus with major uses integrated within one building – it was almost unprecedented. Brunel had in 1839 to realise a new and complex building type for the new railway age. He had to deal with the demands of passengers, their servants, luggage, carriages and horses, railway staff and directors, meeting rooms, waiting rooms and accommodation – but he also, to his mind, had to create architecture – an architecture worthy of the Great Western and the great and epoch-making enterprise upon which it was engaged. As far as Brunel was concerned the terminus had – like the other structures on the line – to possess a nobility that raised railway architecture above mere utilitarian structures. This lofty approach alarmed the directors of the company. They were, in the main, businessmen ultimately looking for profits and here was their engineer – like them a highly practical man when it came to the technology of building a railway – suddenly losing his head over the art of architecture. Time and again Brunel was reined in, like any wayward young artist–architect. In April 1839 his design for Reading Station was rejected by the London Committee of the Great Western which, explained George Gibbs, a member of the Bristol Committee, 'proved to be so far beyond anything we had imagined that we determined . . . not to undertake even a necessary expense, when unexpectedly heavy, without very serious consideration'. The same thing happened again in September 1839 when Brunel's initial Gothic design for the offices at Temple Meads terminus had to be simplified to save costs. Brunel's high-handed behaviour had already led to trouble with the directors of the GWR. In September 1838, during the heated debate over the future of the GWR's broad-gauge track, Brunel was ordered to reduce the expenses of constructing the railway. After a meeting with Brunel on 19 September 1838 Gibbs recorded in his diary that 'we spoke to him very plainly indeed and he expressed himself anxious to co-operate heartily'. Presumably the board spoke to Brunel 'plainly' once again over the extravagance of his architecture and Brunel, ultimately a very sensible fellow, realised that he had better do as his employers directed.

It's the tension between Brunel's two personalities – between the social conservative and the professional radical, between the calculating scientific engineer and the risk-taking, romantic, almost irresponsible artist – that makes him so particularly fascinating. The towering scale of Brunel's achievement as an engineer has tended to dwarf his other creative activities just as his presentation as one of the first modern professionals has obscured the fact that in many respects Brunel belonged, almost as much as did his royalist refugee French father, to the *ancien régime*. But to Brunel's contemporaries the artist Brunel was just as important and admirable as the now more familiar cigar-munching hard-nosed professional engineer. In fact these manifestations were simply seen as two sides of the same coin: essential and complementary expressions of the one great man. In 1870 Brunel's son – Isambard Brunel Junior, published a *Life* of his father. It is a most affectionate portrait, perhaps a little surprisingly so since Brunel was somewhat inadequate as a father – busy, often absent and determined to toughen up the delicate and lame young Isambard by sending him at the age of seven to a stern boarding school. But the book offers a sympathetic portrait, including many memoirs contributed by Brunel's old friends and colleagues. These offer fascinating insights into Brunel's life and interests, and also reveal what his contemporaries valued in him and in his work.

Brunel's friend and brother-in-law – the painter and Royal Academician John Horsley – wrote that Brunel 'being natur-ally imbued with artistic taste and perception of a very high order . . . had a remarkably accurate eye for proportion, as well as taste for form. This is evinced in every line to be found in his sketchbooks, and in all the architectural features of his various works. So small an incident as the choice of colour in the original carriages of the Great Western Railway, and any decorative work called for on the line, gave public evidence of his taste'. This is an extraordinary image. The man who could conceive the modern world in all its pioneering power and glory – vast and ruthlessly engineered bridges of wrought iron and rivets, dark tunnels carved with danger through the bowels of the earth, also chose the colours of his railway carriages and oversaw the minutest decorations of all the trackside architecture.

Brunel relished his role as connoisseur and artist–architect. As Horsley wrote in the *Life*, Brunel passed 'the pleasantest of his leisure moments in decorating [the house in Duke Street], and well do I remember our visits in search of rare furniture, china, bronzes, &c., with which he filled it, till it became one of the most remarkable and attractive houses in London'. Brunel was a veritable powerhouse of creative energy and, in his decoration and architecture as in his engineering, delegated as little as possible to others and certainly made all the key decisions and retained control over all the major phases. G.T. Clark, one of Brunel's engineers, recalled in the *Life* that Brunel had, in all their details, personally designed all the structures along the Great Western route, from the smallest culvert to major works like the Wharncliffe and Maidenhead Viaducts – the latter being a heroic affair – combining a high level of engineering skill with artistic sensibility for its majestic design incorporates the widest, flattest arches ever wrought in brick.

Brunel's working methods as an architect are implied by

several contemporaries. He would produce sketch designs, accurate in scale, form and detail, from which one of his assistants would produce presentation drawings for relevant boards and committees, and then accurate working and detail drawings for estimates and construction. One of the assistants employed to work up and execute Brunel's designs was S.C. Fripp, who was paid three guineas a week for his services. The translation of Brunel's designs into actual buildings was probably a thankless and dispiriting task with any necessary alteration arousing the ire of Brunel who clearly cherished his architectural creations as a father might dote upon a favoured child. Perhaps it is for this reason that the hapless Fripp wearied of his task and eventually enraged Brunel because of his 'abominable & criminal laziness' to the point where Brunel told him to 'pray keep out of my way or I will certainly do you a mischief you have tried my patience so completely'. What a strange little vignette of life in the Brunel office this outburst offers. Brunel – driven and determined to control all – must, for some, have been a hard man to work for, a tough and unrelenting taskmaster. Brunel, motivated by the power of his engineering and architectural visions and a perfectionist packed with creative energy, worked long and exhausting hours himself and expected the same from others, even from humble and less motivated members of staff. Some, like the unfortunate Fripp, were found wanting and soundly chastised. Curiously, Fripp was not dismissed – as a member of a rich Bristol family who were major GWR shareholders this may have proved tricky. But more likely Fripp's survival was due to Brunel's somewhat old-fashioned sense of honour. He might threaten a fellow gentleman with 'mischief' but not sack him.

The architectural manifestations of Brunel's near manic control of building design on the Great Western Railway are gripping and intensely revealing. Brunel had been appointed to survey the route of the Great Western in 1833 and in 1835, after the granting of the Act to build the railway, was made engineer to construct the 118-mile-long track between Paddington and Bristol by way of Reading and Bath. The decade starting in 1829 was one of the most tumultuous and tremendous in British history. In 1829 the Catholic Emancipation Act granted full civil rights to British Roman Catholics; in 1832 the Anatomy Act stopped the grisly practice of body snatching, while the Reform Act of 1832 marked the first step towards universal suffrage; in 1833 all slaves in British possessions were finally emancipated and the Factory Act of the same year ensured that no children under the age of nine should be made to labour in factories. In 1837 Victoria came to the throne and gave her name to an age of power and empire unprecedented in Britain's history. It was a heroic age that demanded heroic characters like Brunel and heroic undertakings such as the rapid construction of Britain's vast and complex railway system.

Within all this social and political change there was also a major change in direction in artistic taste. In a sense morality entered the world of architectural design. During the 1820s British architecture was characterised by rich eclecticism. Greek Classicism had been 'revived' and was a favoured alternative to Roman and Renaissance Classicism, although being challenged by a growing interest in what was called the Italianate style, essentially the inventive Classicism of late Renaissance masters such as Michelangelo. Along with this heady mix of Classical styles there were also exotic essays in the Egyptian, Hindu, Saracenic, Romanesque or Saxon and – of course – all types of Gothic. It was all a matter of taste, often with the same architect producing varied styles to suit the whim of the client or to reflect the function or location of

the building. But during the early 1830s this free and easy
approach to the rich repository of architectural ideas
represented by history was stopped in its tracks. Suddenly
there appeared to be a morally right and wrong way to design.

The man who preached the new morality, with a polemical
passion, was the Roman Catholic convert Augustus Welby
Northmore Pugin. The same age as Dickens and six years
younger than Brunel, Pugin, like Brunel, had a French father
who had fled the Revolution. Pugin preached the virtues of
the Gothic and the villainies of Classical design. Gothic had
evolved for Christian worship, he argued, while Classicism
was pagan in origin but – more important – Gothic was an
advanced engineered architecture, in which all ornament was
essentially a reflection of purpose and structural
requirements, while Classical design was structurally
primitive and limited. In the early 19th century relatively
little was known about the evolution and development of
medieval Gothic architecture and few were capable of
designing in an authentic or archaeologically correct Gothic
manner. Indeed it was only in 1811 that Thomas Rickman
had identified the evolving phases of Gothic architecture and
suggested a chronological development – organised under
the categories of Early English, Decorated and Perpendicular
Gothic – that was essentially correct and which is still in
general use. In these circumstances it is understandable that
Pugin was not entirely correct in his analysis of Gothic – he
simplified issues to make his case – but this was not the
point. He promoted his conviction in dramatically worded
and powerfully illustrated tracts – notably *Contrasts* of 1836
which showed 'the present decay of Taste' in comparison
with the medieval Gothic past, and *The True Principles of
Pointed or Christian Architecture* of 1841. Right or wrong, Pugin
struck a popular chord. He was preaching the return to a

native architecture, Christian in origin, and was proposing a solution to the emerging dilemma of style. The Gothic was, he argued, the artistically and morally appropriate national style for the British nation as it set about establishing itself as the first commercial and imperial power in the world.

This new morality in architecture first manifested itself in a most dramatic manner. In October 1834 the Houses of Parliament – a rambling collection of authentic medieval and modern Classical buildings – were severely damaged by fire. It was soon agreed that they had to be virtually entirely rebuilt and – in June 1835 – a competition was launched to secure a worthy design. One of the stipulations of the brief was that the new design had to be in Gothic or Elizabethan Tudor style because these were perceived to represent the true artistic spirit of Britain. Pugin not only found his theories coinciding with national artistic policy but was hired by Sir Charles Barry – the Classicist architect who won the competition in 1836 – to help in the design of the details for the new Gothic Houses of Parliament. The Gothic that Barry and Pugin chose was that of the late Gothic Perpendicular and Tudor styles. This was partly because they wanted the new Parliament to harmonise with the adjoining and spectacular authentic Perpendicular Gothic of the Henry VII chapel at the east end of Westminster Abbey and partly because Pugin then believed that late Gothic was the ultimate expression of the style – a view he was soon to revise in favour of what he called the Middle Pointed or Decorated Gothic. As the epoch-making 1830s ended what was to become arguably the most important neo-Gothic building in the world got under way, with construction of the foundations commencing in January 1839. It was in this same year that Brunel – who knew the Pugin family and must have followed the debate about the rebuilding of Parliament with intense interest – started to design his own epoch-making building in Bristol, the world's first comprehensively conceived, designed and completed railway terminus.

Brunel's designs for the Great Western terminus at Temple Meads, Bristol, suggests that he was fully aware of the arguments put forward by Pugin while also implying that Brunel was still very much his own man, still a man of the Regency with one foot firmly rooted in the world of Classical design and – contrary to Pugin – a continuing believer in architectural plurality. In 1839 Brunel produced a pair of alternative designs for Temple Meads – one in the Tudor style, the other in the Italian or Classical style. This is no more than was to be expected. In 1827 the young Brunel had become Resident Engineer on his father's Thames Tunnel and so it may have been Isambard who, in the late 1820s or early 1830s, designed the robust Roman Classical architecture that was eventually to grace the tunnel's interior. At roughly the same time he detailed the pylons of his Clifton Suspension Bridge in the Egyptian manner. This happy mix of styles was to characterise Brunel's architectural work on the Great Western Railway. His initial designs of December 1836 for the London terminus at Paddington envisaged an entrance frontage of Roman Classical design while along the route some of the tunnel entrances, such as the west end of the Box Tunnel, were embellished in the Classical manner, while others were decorated with castellated Gothic or Romanesque elevations. The stations were mostly designed in the perpendicular Gothic or Tudor style, no matter what the context.

Brunel's determination to provide the Great Western Railway with ornamental architecture confirms that Brunel saw the creation of a railway system not only as a great commercial and technical undertaking but also as a project with immense artistic potential. The architecture was very much part of his vision of the railways. Although revolutionary, Brunel believed the railway could be rooted in the landscape if its buildings were treated like ornamental structures found in the great estates and parks surrounding country houses. In this fantastical conceit the route of the Great Western was to become the grandest landscaped drive in the world and travelling along it was to offer a picturesque tour through the west of England. To achieve the desired effect Brunel designed his railway architecture in rich and mixed styles so as to create sensations of surprise and pleasure and avoid tedium. Even the most humble structures were to offer delight and evoke pleasant associations. Small stations and trackside buildings were to capture the atmosphere of picturesque garden pavilions, Tudor lodges or fashionable villas while stations were to be designed in the manner of picturesque country houses. For example, the station serving the great Classical city of Bath was built in 1840–1 and is, in appearance, reminiscent of an Elizabethan mansion. Greater works – tunnels and viaducts – designed to conjure up images of ancient Rome or medieval ruins were to impress travellers with a satisfying sense of awe and the sublime. It was a most charming idea and typical of Brunel: a wonderful marriage of the functional and the fantastic, of art with science.

Brunel's idiosyncratic vision of the railway was in harmony with the way the Great Western was originally organised. It was a railway run by and for gentlemen and their ladies and, like most of the early railways, conceived of passenger-carrying trains as a form of transport for the upper classes. Taking its cue from the traditions of the earlier coaching trade, it assumed that poor people wouldn't travel so there were no third-class carriages at first. The first-class carriages had glazed windows and upholstered seats while the second-class carriages, intended for the gentry's servants or tradesmen, had no glass and bare boards. So for the important money-making passengers, travel by train was not only to be quick and reliable but also deeply pleasurable. The journey was to be comfortable, safe, smooth and offer novel and delightful views of the countryside.

Design was also, of course, a question of money. The debate over Temple Meads station is fascinating for it not only reveals a revolutionary building type in the making, but also offers a means of understanding the meaning of the different architectural styles with which Brunel worked. For various bridges in Bristol – such as St Philips Viaduct, the bridge across the River Avon leading to Temple Meads and the bridge across the Floating Harbour – Brunel had worked in a simple Tudor Gothic style using shallow pointed arches. This, of course, reflected the emerging national taste of the moment – inspired by Barry and Pugin in Westminster – but also had practical advantages because a pointed arch is naturally strong.

When designing Temple Meads Brunel wrestled with its practical requirements, such as the functions it should contain and how these functions should be organised in relation to each other. But he also pondered the symbolic purpose. This was to be no merely functional complex. It was to be a work of architecture that reflected the grandeur of the achievement of the Great Western Railway and a celebration of the newly arrived railway age. And this was to be achieved by reference to the past. Brunel, in true Regency rather than modern spirit, eschewed ruthlessly functional design. He could see no merit in creating simple utilitarian architecture in which a visual virtue was made out of the honest expression of function or of materials and means of

construction. He wanted architectural ornament and he
wanted this ornament to carry the pedigree and prestige of
one of the great historic styles. If in his engineering Brunel
was a functionalist pioneer, in his architecture he happily
expressed the aesthetic convictions of the first decades of the
19th century. At the slightly earlier but somewhat disjointed
Euston Station in London, started in 1836, Philip Hardwick
built the sublime Greek Doric propylaeum to serve as the
emblem of the station and to express the glory of railway
travel. Brunel wanted something comparable for the Great
Western and Temple Meads. Rather than create a largely
symbolic structure, Brunel preferred to use the design of the
offices and main entrance as an opportunity to give the
station a grand and ornamental frontage and in May 1839 he
laid his efforts – a pair of alternative designs in different
styles – before the Bristol subcommittee of works.

The committee referred the designs to the Bristol
architect Thomas Foster with instructions to prepare
estimates of the cost of constructing each of the designs.
Foster quickly told the subcommittee that the cost of facing
the Gothic and Italian fronts with Bath stone would cost
£1,379 for the full Gothic treatment, £830 'for a specified
limited' Gothic design and £740 for the Italian design. At its
meeting of 17 May 1839 the subcommittee 'fully considered'
the designs 'submitted by the Engineer for the elevation of
the offices to be created in Temple Meads and also the
estimates prepared by Mr Foster' and resolved 'that the
elevation in the Gothic style be adopted'. This must have
been a most gratifying decision for Brunel. It was also a bold
decision for the subcommittee. Indeed so bold that the
subcommittee felt obliged to justify its actions to the head
office in London. The letter which the Bristol secretary,
Thomas Osler, wrote in July 1839 to his London counterpart

makes gripping reading for, among other things, it explains the significance of the different architectural approaches adopted by Brunel. Osler starts by pointing out that 'Brunel was instructed . . . to prepare plans for . . . offices only as were requisite and which were to be devoid of ornament as was consistent with decent sightlines'. Osler then goes on to explain that 'the first of the sketches exhibited a plain specimen of what I believe is now called the "Tudor" style; the second . . . consisted, I think of as thoroughly naked an assembly of walls and windows as could well be permitted to enclose any Union Poor House in the Country. A single glance at the two seemed to indicate that however agreeable the former might be to our tastes, the latter was the thing for our pockets, but when the Directors placed both Designs in the hands of a leading architect in the place . . . they found, to their surprise, that the cost of the "Tudor" front would exceed that of its Quaker companion by just 90 pounds'. Assuming that this relatively small difference in costs meant that money was not to be the deciding factor in the decision, Osler then lists the artistic and practical advantages of the Gothic design. 'It harmonized not only with the character of the Bridges, Archways &c. already built from Bath westwards, but with the peculiar features of the Gothic specimens of Bristol Architecture'. So Brunel's slightly earlier bridges with their Tudor Gothic arches had established an immediate context for the proposed offices while the city's fine collection of venerable and genuine Gothic buildings were presented as a local precedent for Gothic design. The fact that the vast majority of Bristol's buildings were of Georgian and Regency Classical design is conveniently overlooked. So, in Puginian manner, the implication is that Gothic is morally better, in tune with the true national – and local – style, harmonising with the City's most admirable buildings. Osler's last point suggests the functional superiority of Gothic. The Gothic solution, wrote Osler, 'enables the making of any subsequent additions that may be found necessary . . . without involving violation of symmetry in external Outline as would be inevitable in an Italian design'. So Gothic, as an architecture released from the formal straitjacket of Classical symmetry and naturally responsive to function, was a more flexible style admirably suited to the complex demands of modern uses. Brunel and the subcommittee were allowed their Gothic design, but not before it had been reduced in its scale and ambition to save costs with a simpler design being submitted by Brunel in September 1839. The office was finally built, a rather pinched essay with Tudor Gothic details in an essentially symmetrical, Classical body complete with a Renaissance *piano nobile* – a composite and picturesque product that would have depressed the purist Pugin but typical of the 1830s when the Gothic Revival had not fully arrived at its archaeologically correct phase.

Much more impressive is the train-shed that Brunel designed at Temple Meads. He decided that a great terminus needed a generous covered area where passengers could wait or congregate before boarding and after leaving their trains, and where luggage could be arranged. The platforms at the slightly earlier Euston Station in London had been covered by only a series of small roofs. Brunel resolved on something more ambitious – a vast single-span roof that covered all platforms and tracks. In the 1830s the only prototypes for such constructions were roofs that covered docks and shipbuilding slips. These were invariably engineered in timber with high pitches. In 1839 Brunel set about designing his roof. It was to have a span of 72 feet, achieved with a low pitched roof formed by a series of shallow, pointed Tudor arches. In contrast with Brunel's huge and complex Paddington shed, dating from 1851 and formed with ribs of wrought iron and columns of cast iron, the structure of the Temple Meads shed was largely of timber. In the late 1830s the Victorian iron age had not quite arrived and Brunel, although to become one of the giants of the new age of iron, retained a deep love of timber – of wood, trees and engineered carpentry construction. During his career he designed some remarkable timber trestle viaducts, like that at Gover near St Austell, but the shed roof at Temple Meads is his most ambitious example of timber construction, perhaps inspired by the traditions of the Bristol shipbuilding industry. The light and elegant timber arches seem impossibly shallow and slender for their task – a visual sleight-of-hand achieved through bold engineering skill. Each arch is, in fact, a pair of opposing cantilevers, balanced over the fulcrum point of the cast-iron colonnades above which they span and with their lower ends braced and anchored in the shed's masonry outer walls. Cunningly, Brunel did not allow the top ends of each cantilever to meet because he wanted to avoid the outward thrust that would have been exerted by a true arch. But this clever system got into trouble during construction. The timbers forming the cantilevers started to flex so Brunel bolted wrought-iron plates to the upper and lower faces of the timbers to strengthen them. A brilliant, pragmatic solution that makes the roof a fascinating composite structure.

Brunel's love of timber is another aspect of the central paradox that defines his character and his work. Although forging unprecedented constructions from new materials he retained a love for traditional arts and despite being one of the pioneers of the new industrial, urban world Brunel admired the old ways of country life. As J. C. Horsley explained in the *Life*, Brunel 'displayed a great love of landscape art, and . . . the keenest appreciation of the beauties of nature'. As Brunel was toiling with the technical problems of his Atmospheric Railway in Devon – and facing the prospect of the catastrophic collapse of the entire enterprise – he started to look around for land to buy. He wanted to put down roots in the country and create an estate worthy of a gentleman. 'After a good deal of hesitation', recorded Horsley, 'he fixed upon a spot at Watcombe, about three miles from Torquay . . . He made his first purchase of land in the autumn of 1847; and from that time to within a year of his death the improvement of this property was his chief delight'. This was to be Brunel's paradise on earth. While his health deteriorated and even while he confronted his demons during the plagued project to construct the iron-hulled SS *Great Eastern* – the largest ship the world had ever seen – Brunel expanded and beautified his estate. He became the model landlord – built cottages for his staff and even gave them tickets and a paid holiday to go up to London to visit the Great Exhibition – but mostly he planted trees. 'Assisted by Mr Nesfield, he laid . . . out [the property] in plantations of choice trees. The occupation of arranging them gave him unfailing pleasure . . . there can be little doubt that the happiest hours of his life were spent in walking about in the gardens with his wife and children, and discussing the condition and prospects of his favourite trees'. Discussing the 'prospects' of his trees, as if they were his children – it's a charming image. A house was designed by Brunel – working with William Burn – in the exotic and sumptuous Loire Valley chateau style, well placed, with south-facing terraces, to enjoy vistas to the sea and moor through clumps and avenues of trees.

But Brunel was never to inhabit this magic world, this

romantic realm of his imagination. The stress of completing and launching the SS *Great Eastern* proved too much for his constitution, already weakened by decades of ceaseless toil. He died in September 1859. Only the foundations of his fairy castle had been built and his trees were only just taking root. In 1887 a journalist working for the *Gardeners' Chronicle* went to survey the melancholy scene – an enchanted world which its creator had not lived to enjoy or occupy. 'With one's back to the evening sun,' wrote the journalist, 'the opposite slope presented [a] variety of hues of the evergreens, from the black green of the Austrian pine to the pale tints of the deodars, in contrast with the purple beeches and the light and dark leaves of the other deciduous trees'. The composition was an almost painterly masterpiece in which leaf colours were used as an artist uses pigments. This beautiful landscape, with its subtle and creative manipulation of nature, is a perfect complement to Brunel's nearby iron and powerfully functional Saltash Bridge. Together they reveal the nature of the man – the incredible span of his genius and of his achievements.

1

Isambard Kingdom Brunel was born on 9 April 1806 in a modest terraced house in Britain Street, Portsea, a couple of hundred yards from the Royal Naval Dockyard in Portsmouth. He was the third of three children born to a singularly happy and devoted couple: Marc Isambard Brunel and Sophia Kingdom, who had married on 1 November 1799. They were living in Portsmouth because Marc, probably the most remarkable and able inventor living in Britain at that date, was working on a number of projects for the Royal Navy, including the world's first factory production line: the name of Brunel was becoming well known, if not to the nation at large, then in certain influential quarters.

It was a French name: Brunels had been farming at the hamlet of Hacqueville, a little to the west of Gisors and about halfway between Paris and Rouen, since the 15th century. They were tenant farmers, though tenants of a large and good property, and for several centuries Brunel sons had either taken on the family farm or gone into the Church. Marc Isambard Brunel, born on 25 April 1769, was the third son of Jean Charles and Marie Victoire Brunel, and initially, in his father's eyes, was destined for the Church. He was sent to the college at Gisors, where the pupils wore little cocked hats on their powdered wigs and swords with their military coats, but Marc found that his aptitude and interests lay elsewhere, and by the age of 11 he had announced to his unimpressed father that he wanted to be an engineer. He was sent, nevertheless, to the seminary in Rouen, where the Superior recognised that Marc's talents in woodworking and drawing were of a remarkable order, but his religious vocation was non-existent.

A burgeoning crisis over what Marc was going to do was solved by one of his father's cousins, a Madame Carpentier, who was married to a retired ship's captain who had become the American consul in Rouen. Marc could live with the Carpentiers, and he would attend Rouen's Royal College, where François Jean Noel Dulague, the Professor of Hydrography, agreed to accept him as a pupil (probably on the strength of a good report from the Superior of the seminary). So Marc, aged 13, went to live with the Carpentiers in Rouen, and to study mathematics, geometry, mechanics and drawing. He learned fast, his tutors were impressed, and in 1786, aged 17, he joined a naval frigate as a cadet officer on the new ship *Maréchal de Castries*. It was the start of a six-year career.

Marc returned from a long tour of duty in the Caribbean in January 1792: by this time he was a man of 22, but France was in the throes of revolution, and like his family and like many Normans, he found himself deeply out of sympathy with what was happening in his country. On a visit to Paris in January 1793 he made imprudent remarks critical of the revolutionary leader Robespierre, and was lucky to escape from an angry Jacobin mob. Marc returned to Rouen with his friend François Carpentier, where they found that Mme Carpentier was sheltering an unexpected house guest.

Sophia Kingdom was then 17 years old, youngest of the 16 children of William Kingdom, a naval contractor in Portsmouth. Her father had died some years before and her elder brother, acting as her guardian, had rather imprudently decided that Sophia ought to spend time residing in France to learn the language. So she had come to Rouen with a French friend, a M. de Longuemarre, and his English wife. Only Sophia had fallen ill, and then there had been a terrible incident in which a friend of the de Longuemarres had been murdered by a mob for playing a royalist tune on the piano. Her protectors had fled to England, leaving Sophia staying with Madame Carpentier. Marc and Sophia, both staying under the Carpentiers' roof and both likely to attract the suspicion of the Jacobin government, fell in love. Marc's situation, as a naval officer of royalist sympathies, seemed the more dangerous, and in July 1793 he managed to obtain a passport for the United States, on the pretext of purchasing grain for the navy. After some hazards and adventures, he arrived in New York on 6 September.

While Marc was carving out a new career as a surveyor in New York state, Sophia was in an increasingly perilous situation. At first she taught English to Rouen children, to pay for her board at the Carpentiers. After the execution of Louis XVI, Britain declared war on the new Republic, and in October 1793 British nationals in France were ordered to be imprisoned, and for nine months Sophia was a captive in a makeshift women's prison in a convent at Gravelines, near Calais. A guillotine in the courtyard outside was in frequent use. Petitions were raised by the Carpentiers, and by Republicans whose children she had taught, but it was not until July 1794, when Robespierre himself was overthrown, that Sophia and her fellow captives were released. The Carpentiers nursed her back to health, and in 1795 she obtained a passport to return to England.

Marc spent five and a half years in the United States, working as a surveyor and engineer. His energy and ability won him rapid success, and in the autumn of 1796, after taking American citizenship, he became chief engineer to the city of New York. Indeed, he might very easily have stayed in the United States for good, and it is not altogether clear why he did not. One reason may have been that he had not forgotten Sophia: he had painted her miniature from memory to keep with him, he had regained communication with her, and was writing to her at her family's home in London.

There was also the matter of a business opportunity. One of Marc's most influential American friends was Alexander Hamilton, friend to George Washington and erstwhile first Secretary to the Treasury, an Anglophile with contacts in Britain. At dinner at Hamilton's early in 1798, Marc met a French émigré visitor, a M. Delabigarre, who evidently had some contact with the naval dockyards in England. Perceiving Marc's understanding of ship design, he told him about some of the problems that the navy administration was facing, in particular supply problems to do with ships' rigging blocks. The navy needed a hundred thousand of them a year, they were made by hand, and the supply was too slow. This set Marc to thinking how the manufacture of such an object might be mechanised.

We do not know what the balance of considerations in Marc's mind was from 1798 into 1799. He had been building a considerable name and career for himself in the United States, but by February 1799 he had decided to leave all this behind and start again in England. He took with him 'some small means and many great ideas', and a letter of introduction from his friend Alexander Hamilton to Lord Spencer, Secretary for the Navy in William Pitt's government.

Marc arrived in Falmouth on 13 March 1799, and made his way to London, where he took rooms in Stoke Newington. He swiftly introduced himself to the Kingdom family and renewed his acquaintance with Sophia. He was then approaching 30 and she was 24, and it may be that she was the real reason that Marc had left the United States, for by the summer they had announced their engagement. They were married at her family's parish church of St Andrew, Holborn, on 1 November 1799, and they set up house in Bedford Street in Bloomsbury.

Marc had to establish his name all over again from scratch, but he had come to England equipped with ideas, and within a month of his arrival he had filed the first of an eventual 17 patents – for a 'duplicating writing and drawing machine' or polygraph. The big opportunity, though, seemed to be in addressing the navy's need for the more efficient production of rigging blocks. These were made, by hand, by a firm of contractors called Fox & Taylor. A rigging block consisted, in essence, of a shell – hollowed out from a solid block of oak – within which sat a pulley wheel or sheave, fitted with a bearing of bell metal so that it could turn on an iron pin, slotted through the shell. A 74-gun ship needed 922 blocks, the blocks got worn out in use, and the Royal Navy needed a hundred thousand of them a year, for which it was paying about £24,000 per annum. Marc's insight was that if a system of mass production could be devised, thousands of pounds a year would be saved. Throughout 1800 he was working up his designs for such a system.

In 1799 Marc was introduced to a mechanic, Henry Maudslay, who had premises on Wells Street, just north of Oxford Street and a few hundred yards from Bedford Street. Maudslay was then 28 years old and had served an apprenticeship with Joseph Bramah, celebrated locksmith and engineer, but had left to set up on his own the previous year. He became the greatest mechanical engineer of the age, his planes, lathes and steam engines among the finest yet produced. If anyone could realise Marc's ideas, Maudslay could. Early in 1801 he finished the first models of Marc's machines, and in February, Marc filed for his second patent. He tried taking this to Fox & Taylor, whose workforce of over a hundred made the blocks by hand in Southampton, but they rejected his approach, claiming to have achieved the perfect production process already.

At this point, two key individuals came to Marc's assistance. One was George, 2nd Earl Spencer, until recently the Navy Secretary in Pitt's government, to whom Hamilton had written his letter of introduction. Spencer was highly cultivated and interested in the sciences, and was impressed by his visitor: he was to be one of Marc's most loyal and effective friends. Lord Spencer introduced him to Sir Samuel Bentham, brother of the philosopher Jeremy and Inspector General of Naval Works, and a most formidable figure. He had returned to Britain in 1791 after several years working in Russia, and from his appointment as Inspector General in 1796 Bentham had imposed a thorough overhaul of the naval dockyards. One of his great interests was in the mechanisation of the processes for handling and cutting the huge quantities of timber used in the dockyards: Marc's invention was exactly the kind of thing he was looking for. Bentham was the ideal patron, and like Earl Spencer, he was to be Marc's friend for life.

On 15 April 1802, Bentham recommended the installation of Brunel's and Maudslay's block-making machines at Portsmouth.

Marc and Sophia had been living off the money he had saved in America, a lot of which had had to be sunk into the development of the block machines, but in the previous year he and Maudslay had developed and refined the inventions to a remarkable degree. By the end of 1802 the Brunels had moved to the house in Britain Street, Portsea, so that Marc could oversee the installation of the first production line. This was in operation by 1803, and by 1805 two further production lines had been installed and commissioned: a total of 45 Brunel and Maudslay machines. There were drills to cut holes for the block pins, saws to trim the corners, mortising machines with chisels to cut out the slot for the pulley, shaping machines to plane the sides of the block to the requisite curved profiles, scoring machines to cut grooves in the sides, saws to cut the coak or pulley out of *lignum vitae*, and a further series of lathes and milling machines to finish the pulleys. A 12-horsepower engine to power the machines soon had to be replaced by a 30-horsepower engine.

This summary hardly does justice to the integrated efficiency and precision of the process, or to its implications. Suddenly, 10 unskilled hands could produce as many perfect blocks as 110 craftsmen in Fox & Taylor's workshop. The latter firm paid a heavy price for their complacency, losing their contract in 1805. Marc could not have chosen a better collaborator: Maudslay's machines were so well made that most of them were still in production in the 20th century: landing craft on D-Day in 1944 were equipped with blocks made on their production line. The implications went much wider than block-making: Brunel and Maudslay had demonstrated that machines, adapted to perform specific tasks and arranged in a production line, manned by relatively unskilled workers, could vastly out-produce traditional craft production. There was a clear analogy with the transition from handloom weaving to powered looms which was already taking place in the north of England. The machine-tool industry had been born.

While Marc was installing his machines in the Royal Dockyard, his family was growing: two daughters, Sophia and Emma, had been born in 1801 and 1804 respectively, and in 1806, as Marc recorded in his journal:

> On the 9th of April, at five minutes before one o'clock in the morning, my dear Sophia was brought to bed of a boy.

The block mill was now in production and Marc's business interests were shifting to London, so in the summer of 1807 he moved his family to No. 4 Lindsey Row, Chelsea, one of seven houses converted out of a fine 17th-century mansion, Lindsey House. It was there that Isambard spent his childhood, surrounded by a loving family with a wide circle of friends. Marc doted on his little son, teaching him arithmetic and drawing, and explaining to him how machines worked. In 1813, aged eight, Isambard went to a nearby day school run by the Reverend Weedon Butler: he was already displaying great gifts both for drawing and mathematics, and before long he was sent to a more demanding boarding establishment run by a Dr Morrell, in Hove. This was a progressive school by the standards of the day, and Isambard studied modern languages, as well as Latin and Greek. A letter to his mother, written from Dr Morrell's school when he was 13, gives some idea of his lively, precocious personality:

> I like Horace very much, but not as much as Virgil. As to what I am about, I have been making half a dozen boats lately, till I have worn my hands to pieces. I have also taken a plan of Hove, which is a very amusing job. I should be much obliged if you would ask Papa (I hope he is quite well and

hearty) whether he would lend me his long measure. It is a long eighty-foot tape; he will know what I mean. I will take care of it, for I want to make a more exact plan, though this is pretty exact, I think. I have been drawing a little . . .

Marc's career had broadened out, after the five or so years of intensive work to get the block mills into production, into several other areas: the range of his activity and invention was remarkable. First, in the period 1805–10, he put the experience gained from developing the block mills into a series of powered saws, much of this being done in collaboration with Maudslay. Marc developed great circular, steam-powered saws for cutting up timber in bulk, stave-cutting saws to improve barrel manufacture, and a machine for cutting wood into thin veneers. Circular saws made to Marc's designs were installed in the Portsmouth dockyard, and in October 1806 he formed a partnership with a Mr Farthing to establish a private business, a sawmill in Battersea: it was to supervise this that Marc had moved himself and his family back to London. Marc supplied the technology and his partner the capital: fortunately, Farthing was honest as well as capable, and the Battersea mill grew into a strong and profitable business.

This was as well, for Marc himself was no businessman, always finding it very difficult to concentrate on money issues. Besides, the Navy Board were proving slow to reward him for his efforts on their behalf: the agreement had been that he would be paid an allowance of a guinea a day while working for the navy, and that when his equipment was installed and proved he should receive a sum equivalent to the saving made by his block machines in a year. Marc had had to spend over £2,000 of his own money – far more than the allowance – in developing the machinery, and it was not until the summer of 1809 that the main sum due to him, over £17,000, was paid.

In February 1809 Marc had been in Portsmouth, visiting his
new sawmill in the dockyard: he saw the veterans of the
Corunna campaign disembarking and was shocked by their
condition, in particular by the number of them that had no
boots, only filthy rags binding their feet. Marc made enquiries:
he found that the army spent £150,000 a year on boots, but
according to the soldiers, the boots seemed to wear out in no
time. Marc bought a few pairs, cut them up, and found out the
secrets of their cheap, skimped construction: the soles were
made of thin sheets of leather, with a layer of clay packed
between to make up the bulk. His inventor's mind turned over
the matter, and by August 1810 he had filed another patent
simply entitled 'Shoes and Boots', for a system of mass
production. This time, Marc decided, it would be a private
venture. He and Farthing set up a factory near the Battersea
sawmill, employing 24 disabled soldiers to operate machines
which produced strong boots and shoes in nine different sizes.
The boot factory, like the sawmill, attracted influential visitors,
among them Lord Castlereagh. In 1812 Brunel and Farthing
became the principal contractors to the army, and their
production rose to 400 pairs a day: many of Wellington's army
at Waterloo were wearing Brunel boots. The Iron Duke's own
opinion is not recorded, but with his celebrated eye for detail it
seems likely that he would have known who was responsible for
the improvement in the army's footwear. Certainly, the Duke
was to be one of Marc's most important supporters in the
difficulties that lay ahead.

Marc had become a major contractor to the government, and
supporter of Britain's war effort. He had installed a frame-saw
mill in the carriage factory at the Royal Arsenal, Woolwich. In
1812–13 he designed and installed a log-handling and timber-
cutting sawmill in the dockyard at Chatham (a curious point
about this was that the rope-hauled railway which delivered the

sawn planks to the seasoning yard had rails seven feet apart: Marc had pioneered what later became known as the 'broad gauge', more usually attributed to his son). By the time the Chatham mill was up and running, with his customary enthusiasm for a new field of enquiry, Marc was investigating the application of steam power to shipping. He designed and commissioned a special double-acting steam engine (an engine with two pistons, which worked in alternation to turn an axle), and had it installed in a packetboat, the *Regent*. The little boat was a great success, providing ferry services between London and Margate.

In 1812–13 his businesses were thriving: the Battersea sawmill returned a profit of £8,000 a year. However, there were danger signs as well. Marc spent heavily from his own resources on his inventions, and was inclined to neglect business. While Farthing was managing this side of things, matters proceeded well enough, but Farthing retired in 1813. On 30 August 1814 the sawmill at Battersea was destroyed in a great fire: Marc investigated his bank account, which the previous October had held £10,000, and found the balance standing at £865. Then the boot factory ran into heavy losses, as the government ran the army down after the victory at Waterloo in June 1815: Marc was urged to continue production and did so, but without being given any firm order. By the autumn he had £5,000-worth of unsold boots, which had to be sold at clearance prices to pay for re-equipping the sawmill. This was the reward for his contribution to victory.

During the years 1816–21, while Isambard was at home in Lindsey Row or at school with Dr Morrell in Hove, Marc produced a stream of designs and inventions. There was a *tricoteur* or knitting machine, which worked but didn't sell, as woven cotton from Lancashire was still cheaper than knitted woollen hose. There was a commission to design a water-supply system for Paris, which was supported by Louis XVIII, but failed because of the opposition of the city's water-porters. Then there was a commission from Tsar Alexander I to design a crossing of the River Neva at St Petersburg. Marc toyed with the idea of a tunnel, puzzling for the first time over the problems of how to tunnel through soft ground beneath a great body of water. He abandoned this in favour of a bridge, conceiving one design for a timber arch 800 feet in span, and another design for a kind of suspension bridge with a central tower (for comparison, Telford's Menai suspension bridge of 1819–26, then just designed, has a clear span of 600 feet). Marc sent his designs via the Russian ambassador, Prince Lieven, but the Tsar's treasurers balked at the cost. Much of Marc's energy was being invested in ideas that wouldn't run.

The Brunels had become well connected and well known. Marc had been elected to the Royal Society in 1814, and his circle of friends included such eminent figures as Charles Babbage, inventor of the first 'calculating engine' or computer, the chemist Sir Humphry Davy, and Michael Faraday, scientist and pioneer of the use of electricity. Earl Spencer was among his close friends, and the Brunels were guests at Spencer House and at Althorp, their country house in Northamptonshire. On Sundays the Brunels went to visit their friends the Hawes family in Lambeth: Sophia Brunel became engaged to their elder son Benjamin, while their younger son William was then Isambard's closest friend.

In 1820 Isambard, then aged 14, finished at Dr Morrell's school and was sent to study in France, first at Caen College, then at the Lycée Henri IV in Paris. It was a specialist school which gave pupils an education in science and mathematics as a preparation for the École Polytechnique: Marc knew that there was no formal schooling available in Britain which could compare with that provided at the Henri IV, and it is faintly ironic that it had been established by the Napoleonic regime to whose overthrow he had made such important contributions. Isambard did well there and might have entered the École Polytechnique itself, but was barred from doing so by his foreign birth. Instead, he entered the workshop of the famous clockmaker Louis Breguet as an apprentice, living in his family home.

His father, meanwhile, continued to be as inventive as ever. In 1818–20, he devised a new way of making a decorative packaging from tinfoil and invented a hand-held copying press, which could take single copies from a document written in ink. He started work on an altogether more complex project to develop a rotary press suitable for printing newspapers with the backing of John Walter, son of the proprietor of *The Times*. However, Marc's inattention to business, and the large sums he was sinking in his inventions without due regard to what hope there was (if any) of a financial return, were about to catch up with him. The profits from the sawmill were being swallowed up elsewhere, while the boot factory had ceased to make profits, and the decorative tinfoil process was pirated. In the spring of 1821 his bankers, Sykes & Company, became insolvent. No one would honour Marc's cheques now, but the bills kept coming in and on 18 May 1821 the unthinkable happened: he and Sophia were arrested for debt and consigned to the King's Bench Prison in Southwark. Isambard was in Paris, staying with Breguet and his family.

Marc reflected bitterly on the government's apparent indifference to his fate, after all his services to the British nation. He wrote to influential friends, including Earl Spencer. After ten weeks of humiliating confinement, more drastic action seemed in order. Marc let it be known that he had resumed contact with Tsar Alexander I, who had once made generous expressions of support. The thought that he might be lost to

the country sent ripples through Whitehall and the Duke of
Wellington asked what steps the Chancellor of the Exchequer
was taking to ensure that Mr Brunel's services were retained for
the nation. After a couple more weeks of wrangling, a Treasury
grant of £5,000 was agreed. A deputation, including Admiral
Sir Edward Codrington, set out for the King's Bench. Sir Edward
later recollected the circumstances in which he first met Marc:

> On visiting the prison, the deputation was ushered into a
> small room, in one corner of which was Brunel at a table
> littered with papers, covered with mathematical calculations
> while, seated on a trestle bed in the opposite corner of the
> room sat his wife, mending his stockings. There, under those
> painful circumstances, I first made his acquaintance, and now
> you see him, my most honoured guest.

Marc and Sophia returned home early in August: one of the first
things he did was to write a letter of thanks to the Duke of
Wellington. He sold the boot and tinfoil businesses, and re-
established the Battersea sawmill with new partners, two
brothers named Hollingsworth, and a cousin of Sophia's named
Mudge.

A year later, in August 1822, Isambard returned from France
and started work in his father's office: the staff then probably
consisted of Marc, aged 54; Isambard, aged 16, and a clerk. Work
poured in and over the next couple of years Marc and Isambard
worked together on designs for a cannon-boring mill for the
Dutch government, the rotary newspaper printing press, paddle
tugs for the River Rhine, a sawmill on the island of Trinidad,
and much else besides: no better education for an engineer could
have been devised. The French government commissioned
designs for two suspension bridges for the Île de Bourbon off
Mauritius, the island now called Réunion: the smaller St

Suzanne bridge was to have a single span of 131 feet 9 inches between twin towers, while the bridge on the River du Mât was to have twin spans of the same length to either side of a central tower. Marc had to make several journeys to visit the contractors, the Milton Ironworks at Sheffield, before a trial erection could take place, after which the chains had to be taken to London for testing. At length, on 29 November, the ironwork was despatched by ship from Gravesend.

Marc also resumed his experiments in mechanical engineering, and Isambard was deeply involved in this, too. In 1822 he registered another patent, called 'Certain Improvements in Steam Engines'. The lessons learned from the steam packet *Regent* were put to use in a visionary design for a marine engine in the form of an inverted 'V' with many innovative features: his design later formed the basis for Isambard's much larger engines for the *Great Britain*.

On 30 May 1823, Marc noted in his diary:

Met Sir H. Davy, who adverted to the discovery of a carbonic gas to be used as a power – which he denominates a differential power.

This was the start of a long campaign, which absorbed much of Isambard's time and Marc's money over the next ten years, to develop a 'Gaz Engine'. Humphry Davy and Michael Faraday had discovered that a number of gases could be liquefied by a combination of low temperature and very high pressure: by raising the temperature one could return them to a gaseous state, and by lowering the temperature again, the gas could be made to condense and re-liquefy. Marc became convinced that this could be the basis for a new and more efficient kind of engine: he produced a design in which a double-acting piston (one pushed alternately from either end) moved back and forth in an oil-filled metal cylinder. This was flanked by two pairs of pressure vessels: one of each pair was filled with pressurised carbonic gas, while the other was filled with oil as a medium for transferring changes of pressure. The idea was that, in alternation, one gas cylinder would be heated up (with hot water passed through tubes), causing the gas to return to a gaseous state (i.e. expand), while the other cylinder was cooled (again with water) to freezing point, causing the gas to condense and liquefy. Changing the state of the gas in the two cylinders in alternation created a pressure differential. This would drive the piston up and down, which could (in theory, at any rate) be used to turn an axle, which could be geared up to drive an engine. So for the rest of the 1820s, Isambard spent much of his time working with pressurised carbonic gas and achieving hair-raisingly high pressures, ranging from 30 to 100 atmospheres (that is, up to 1,400 pounds per square inch) as the gas alternately condensed and expanded. There were occasional mishaps and it is a marvel, or perhaps it is a tribute to Marc's and Isambard's skill, that no one was injured. Marc was quite convinced that it would succeed: after all, it was based on the work of his friends Davy and Faraday, the most eminent chemists of the age. He sank over £15,000 of his own money (and £200 of the Admiralty's money) in to the project, but for whatever reason, the Gaz Engine could not be made to work.

In the same summer of 1823, Marc had also begun work on the project for which he is best-known, which was to dominate the rest of his life: the Thames Tunnel. London, by then, had long been established as the greatest port and commercial centre in the world, but the Thames, which was its origin and its basis, was also a great barrier to communication between the north and south banks. Getting a coach or a loaded cart through the narrow streets and across the traffic bottleneck of London Bridge could be a very slow business. This concerned the government, too: if a foreign invader were to come up the Thames estuary, then getting defending troops from the north bank to the south (or vice versa) could be a difficult proposition. Yet a bridge, anywhere below London Bridge, would surely represent an unacceptable obstacle to shipping.

This problem had already inspired two initiatives. In May 1798 a surveyor named Ralph Dodd established a company and began to raise investment for a 900-yard tunnel between Tilbury and Gravesend. Dodd's estimate of £15,995 must have seemed extraordinarily optimistic, and when he sank a shaft he did not find the continuous bed of chalk that he had hoped for. If a fire in the engine house hadn't finished off his venture, then the geology of the Thames estuary would surely have done so.

A second and much more credible attempt was made by a Cornish mining engineer called Robert Vazie. He had experience of digging out below the sea, and he proposed to take a drift (that is, a tunnel about three feet square) through the river bed, and use that as the starting point and drain for a brick-lined tunnel above it. A company was set up, and a shaft was dug which promptly flooded, and Vazie was supplanted by his fellow Cornishman Richard Trevithick. In 1807 Trevithick and a band of miners pushed the drift over a thousand feet, almost across the river, before it flooded again. Trevithick barely escaped with his life and the Thames Archway Company folded.

Marc pondered this problem from time to time over the following years. The bed of the Thames and the strata beneath it were not formed of reassuringly solid rock, but of mud, gravel, clay and quicksand. How could a tunnel be dug safely through such treacherously soft ground, if the weight of the river above constantly threatened to bring the tunnel roof – closely followed by hundreds of tons of water – down on the miners' heads, before they could construct a solid lining? One day in 1816, inspecting his sawmill at Chatham Dockyard, Marc came across a piece of old timber removed from a ship, pitted with wormholes. He took out his eyeglass, and found in it a live ship worm, a *Teredo navalis*, an enemy to all sailors and shipwrights. This simple mollusc, about nine inches long, has a soft, semi-transparent body, but its head is encased in two triangular shells, between which there is a proboscis. The shells rotate about the proboscis, grinding the timber immediately ahead of it to a powder fine enough for the worm to eat. From this monotonous diet the worm produces a layer of excreta, which petrifies and lines the tunnel that it cuts for itself. An idea began to form in Marc's mind, and although he did not patent it until 1818, and did not finalise the design for his 'Great Shield' until 1823, this was, by his own testimony, the origin of the idea which led to the construction of the Thames Tunnel and, in due course, the development of modern tunnel engineering.

2

From London to Bristol

The story of the construction of the Thames Tunnel, the first tunnel ever to be driven beneath a major body of water, is one of the epics of engineering history. It played a pivotal role in the lives of the Brunels, father and son, effectively concluding Marc's career in an immensely drawn-out final act, and starting Isambard's – though for a good while it looked as if it had been a false start.

Marc's period of enforced leisure in the King's Bench Prison afforded him some thinking time, and he devoted some of it to the problems that Vazie and Trevithick had faced in driving their 'drift' beneath the Thames. The strata were deeply problematic. Under the river and beneath the mud there was a bed of gravel, which went to 40 feet or so below the land surface. Below this, Vazie had found a band of firmer ground, which he estimated to be 34 feet deep. Below this, at 76 feet, he had hit a deep layer of quicksand, full of water at some pressure. In general terms, the problem was this: he couldn't go through the gravel layer, it being unstable and directly beneath the water; he couldn't go down into the quicksand either, as the workings would be flooded and the miners might sink without trace: a tunnel could only be driven through the layer between. Geologically speaking, he was between Scylla and Charybdis. This is why the optimal design for the tunnel turned out to have its roof a mere 14 feet below the river bed at the mid-point. With hindsight we can see that the tunnel was, in fact, just barely achievable given the geology, materials and technology at his disposal, but Marc could not know how much of an ordeal it was going to be, and if he had known, the tunnel would probably not have been built.

The geology helped determine the design of the tunnel. In his 1818 patent Marc had made the tunnel and tunnelling shield cylindrical. Once he understood how soft the ground conditions would be, he realised that it would be difficult to support the tunnel roof given such a shape. In September 1823 he published an article in the *Mechanic's Magazine*, describing a rectangular tunnelling shield much like the one he eventually used. By this time he had worked out the whole design. He would sink a shaft on the south bank at Rotherhithe, about 70 feet deep and lined with brick. From here, the miners would drive the tunnelling shield northwards beneath the bed of the river for 1,250 feet, while a team of bricklayers constructed a massive lining forming twin tunnels, behind them. By the time that they reached the north bank at Wapping the northern shaft would have been sunk, in time for the tunnel to link up with it. The two shafts would house access stairs for foot passengers, and in due course Marc intended to build circular ramps or 'Great Descents' at either end, for horses, carriages and carts. It was a complete plan with quantities and estimates, and he began to look for support for his great vision.

From February 1824 the pace of events quickened. Expressions of support were coming in from money men, fellow engineers and the dock companies. William Smith, MP for Norwich, offered to act as chairman, and on 18 February an inaugural public meeting was held to set up a company. A parliamentary bill, sanctioning the scheme and empowering them to levy tolls at fixed rates, went through remarkably quickly, receiving royal assent on 24 June. The first general meeting of the Thames Tunnel Company, with William Smith in the chair, was held on 20 July: Marc was offered £5,000 for the use of his patent at the outset with another £5,000 when the tunnel was complete, and a salary of £1,000 a year for three years to act as the company's engineer. By this time he had leased land in Rotherhithe and carried out surveys, and on 11 June 1824 he closed up both his office in Poultry and the family home at Lindsey Row, and moved both to 30 Bridge Street, Blackfriars, so as to be closer to the scene of his labours. Marc still had other business to manage, there was much preparatory work to do, and it was not until 2 March 1825 that the first stone of the Rotherhithe shaft was laid.

Isambard was then 19, one of five staff employed in his father's office, paid £12 10s. per quarter. Like his father he was keeping a journal, but unlike his father's, which was largely a record of business, Isambard's was highly personal in character. This was his entry for 9 March 1825, just a week after the foundation ceremony in Rotherhithe:

> Projects are on foot for Fowey and Padstow Canal and the Bermondsey Docks. I am preparing plans for South London Docks – in case my father should be named Engineer. I am very busily engaged with the Gaz Engine, and a project is likewise made for a canal across the Panama. Surely one of these may take place.
>
> It may be curious at some future date to read the state we are in at present – I am most terribly pinched for money. Should receive barely enough next quarter to pay my debts, and am, at this moment, without a penny. We keep neither carriage, nor horse, nor footman, only two maid-servants. I am looking forward with great anxiety to this Gaz Engine – building castles in the air about steam boats that go fifteen miles per hour; going on a tour to Italy; being the first to go to the West Indies, and making a large fortune, building a house for myself, etc. etc. How much more likely it is that all this will turn out to nothing! The Gaz Engine, if it is good for anything, will only be tolerably good, and perhaps make us spend a good deal of money; that I should pass through life as most people, and that I should gradually forget my castles in the air, live in a small house, and, at most, keep my gig. On the other side, it may be much worse. My father may die, or the Tunnel may fail, and I most likely in such circumstances, cut my throat or hang myself. But whatever may turn out, I should, in imagination, have enjoyed my fortune for at least a year or two without doing anybody harm.

Isambard's writing, always vivid and direct, conveys both his ambition and his frustration. Reading this, the motivation behind his amazing capacity for work becomes a little clearer.

To make the tunnel, Marc needed to start by building a shaft, and this had to be 50 feet in diameter and 70 feet deep: how could such a thing be dug without flooding, or collapsing, or both? He designed a cast-iron ring, made in 48 segments, 50 feet in diameter. It had a cutting edge on its lower side, and an upper flange or shelf, 10 inches wide. The ring was assembled on the site of the shaft. 24 short piles were driven into the ground in a circle just inside it. A timber curb or shelf was built, spanning from the piles to the iron ring. This structure was loaded with bricks and left to settle for a week or so, then bricklayers started building a brick tower, on top of the timber curb. They raised a yard-thick wall to a height of 35 feet in three weeks and faced it with Roman cement (which, despite its name, was a recently invented material, very hard and waterproof). Carpenters made a timber platform on top of the tower, and a hand windlass was set up, an interim measure while they were waiting for a steam engine to power a bucket chain. The timber piles (which had been put there to ensure that the structure remained stable at its maximum height) were removed. Then workmen started removing the earth inside the tower: the iron ring cut into the soft ground, and the structure sank evenly by eight inches on the first day. The sinking tower of Rotherhithe became one of the sights of London, and was visited by the Duke of Wellington and General Ponsonby on 22 April. By early June, the tower/shaft had sunk to its prescribed depth, and Marc was preparing to underpin it with a strong brick floor with a central cistern for drainage, dug further down into the ground. There were some tricky moments, given the uneven ground and the ever-present water, but in October the shaft was finished, and a wide opening was formed in its north face. Maudslay delivered the sections of Marc's 'Great Shield', 36 feet wide and 21 feet 4 inches high, which fitted neatly into this opening. Tunnelling began on 28 November 1825.

Marc's plan was that his miners would work within 12 iron frames side by side, each in three storeys, making a total of 36 working positions. Ahead of each miner was a row of horizontal 'poling boards', behind which was the working face. The method, stated very simply, was for each miner to remove the poling boards in front of him one at a time, dig out four inches of ground, then replace the board, screwed forward. When the three miners in a frame had 'worked down' all their boards, their frame was pushed forward with screw jacks: the odd-numbered frames were worked forward, then the even-numbered ones, in alternation. The Shield stood on substantial feet to keep it even, and it had a solid cast-iron roof and substantial side panels to hold back the soft, potentially treacherous ground. Each time it moved forward a team of bricklayers extended the tunnel lining, a massive double-tube of brickwork. The overall cross-section was rectangular – the same size and shape as the Shield, of course – forming twin horseshoe-shaped tunnels. The Shield's screw jacks had to be braced against the leading edge of the most newly laid brickwork. A moving platform, just behind the Shield, enabled the spoil to be removed. Marc must have worked out a fairly complex sequence for all these processes to have meshed together.

It was a slow and laborious business: it took over a month just to work the Shield through the side of the Rotherhithe shaft, and get it into uniform contact with the earth. Marc and the Company had envisaged that the tunnel would be finished in three years: 400 feet a year, eight feet a week. In fact, the first eight feet had taken a month, but by the spring of 1826 the miners were learning how to use the Shield, and had established a working rhythm.

Marc had fallen ill with pleurisy about the time that tunnelling started, and the first Resident Engineer, John

Armstrong, did not last long, resigning in August 1826. After that, the work was run on a daily basis by an ex-guardsman, Richard Beamish; William Gravatt, mathematician and son of an instructor at the Royal Artillery's Academy at Woolwich; and Isambard. From the borehole survey, it was thought that there was a continuous layer of good clay, about three feet deep and just above their working level, which would provide a waterproof 'ceiling', but as the miners inched forward the strata became more complex, and the ground wetter. At first the work was lit by candles, but from March 1826 Marc introduced lamps lit from gas canisters. The men laboured away, two shifts a day for eight hours each in this dim light, in an atmosphere which became fouler the further they advanced. Periodically, water poured through the boards and threatened to flood the tunnel, or the work threatened to go off line, or sections of the Shield broke, or men fell ill from the foul atmosphere. Throughout 1826 the Brunels, Beamish and Gravatt contended with these problems, while also coping with critical, penny-pinching directors, and with understandable outbreaks of drunkenness and obstreperousness from their workforce. By the end of the year they had advanced 350 feet.

On 3 January, at his father's proposal, Isambard was appointed Resident Engineer at a salary of £200 per annum, with Gravatt, Beamish and a newcomer, Riley, as assistants. This reflected his efforts at the work face, leading and motivating. During a particularly bad crisis in September 1826, Beamish had endured two spells of duty lasting 53 hours and 20 hours, separated by one day – but Isambard remained in the works for five days in succession without ascending, snatching brief naps on the spoil platform. His new authority was immediately put to the test: the board reduced the miners' wages to 2s 10d. per day, and a few days later he was obliged to face down a strike.

In the spring of 1827 the western arch of the tunnel was rendered, decorated and opened to the public: Marc had devised a simple but handsome classical treatment, with arches decorated with Doric semi-columns in the dividing wall. As many as 700 visitors a day paid a shilling to see the work, but the tunnel was now under the middle of the river and conditions were becoming even more dangerous. The ground they were going through had become quite extraordinarily disgusting: the Thames had been London's main sewer and refuse dump for the past thousand years. Men fainted at the Shield face, and were carried off suffering from dizziness, chest pains, impaired vision and suppurating arms. Isambard spent his 21st birthday, 9 April 1827, at work, where he sacked three discontented miners. Water came through the roof on 21 April, bringing with it gravel, coal, bones and pieces of china from the river bed. What had happened to the three feet of protective clay? Isambard hired a diving bell to inspect the bed of the river: a depression had appeared above the Shield, which was now covered by so little that, from the bell, they could tap its surface with an iron rod, then push an iron tube through the mud and hold a conversation with a miner standing in it. Isambard took various people, including his mother and her friend Mrs Baldwin, down in the diving bell, but despite this insouciance, he must have known that they were on the brink of disaster. On 17 May the silt turned liquid, 'the ground seemed as though it were alive', and the river burst in, washing hundreds of tons of mud into the tunnel.

Isambard hired the diving bell to explore the river bed again: a crater 50 feet across and nine feet deep had appeared above the breach. By late June they had dumped huge quantities of bagged clay into the crater and half pumped out the tunnel. Isambard and three others rowed along the tunnel and crawled along the top of the mudbank to inspect the damage to the Shield.

Herculean labours were required to clear the tunnel and mend the Shield, and it was not until October that they were inching forward again. On 7 October, at night, Isambard fell into a water tank in the works yard whose cover had been left open: he was badly injured and was off work for a couple of weeks. In November he was back, and on the 10th he presided at a grand banquet held in the tunnel, which was draped in crimson and lit with candelabra for the occasion, while the sound of the band of the Coldstream Guards (Beamish's old regiment) crashed and echoed around them. While Isambard, the directors and their guests dined in the eastern arch, 120 workmen were dining in the western arch, and after dinner they drank the young Resident Engineer's health and presented him with a pick and shovel.

The banquet was a magnificent display of bravado, but the Thames was as close as ever. Working conditions were appalling, the ground was soft silt, and on 11 January the river burst in again. Isambard, on duty, was very nearly drowned. He was carried, unconscious, by a wave of water pouring up the tunnel, and rescued in the nick of time by Beamish. Six less fortunate men were drowned that night. Isambard was carried home:

> Never felt so queer, could not bear the least shake, felt as if I should be broken to pieces . . .

Isambard was seriously ill, suffering from haemorrhaging for some months to come. He went to Brighton to convalesce, then in April he was back with his parents in Blackfriars:

> Here I am in bed at Bridge House. I have now been laid up useless since 12 January. I shan't forget that day in a hurry. Very near finished my journey then. When the danger is over it is amusing rather than otherwise . . . When knocked down

I certainly gave myself up, for I never expected we should get out. The roar of the water in a confined space was very grand, cannon can be nothing to it. Apart from the loss of those six poor fellows the whole affair was well worth the risk, and I would willingly pay my share of the expenses.

Meanwhile, the Thames Tunnel's workmen were filling in the breach in the river bed with bags of clay again, and by April they were well on the way to clearing the tunnel for the second time, but this new disaster had driven the Company into financial crisis. While his father wrangled with the directors, Isambard wondered about the tunnel's future – and his own:

The young Rennies, whatever their real merit, will have built London Bridge, the finest bridge in Europe . . . Palmer has built new London Docks and thus without labour has established a connexion which ensures his fortune, while I shall have been engaged on the Tunnel which failed, which was abandoned – a pretty recommendation.

I have nothing after all so very transcendent as to enable me to rise by my own merit without some such help as the Tunnel. It's a gloomy perspective and yet bad as it is I cannot with all my efforts work myself up to be down hearted. Well, it's very fortunate I am so easily pleased. After all let the worst happen – unemployed, untalked of, penniless (that's damned awkward) I think I may depend upon a home at Benjamin's. My poor father would hardly survive the tunnel. My mother would follow him. I should be left alone – here my invention fails, what would follow I cannot guess . . .

This was on 7 May 1828. By August the Shield was cleared – and bricked up. The workmen were paid off, the tunnel was cleaned up, a giant mirror was erected at the far end and it was opened to the public. Marc's great vision seemed to have failed, just as Isambard feared. Isambard's diaries and correspondence become thinner at this point: according to his son's biography, he spent the rest of 1828 and most of 1829 occupied in scientific researches in collaboration with Charles Babbage and Michael Faraday. We do not know quite why he went to Bristol in the first place in 1829, but it turned out to be a providential decision.

Bristol had been a major port city since the Middle Ages and had for long prided itself on being the 'second city in England'. In the 18th century its merchants and bankers had played a major part in developing the 'triangular trade'. Their ships took English manufactured goods to West Africa for sale; the proceeds were used to buy slaves who were shipped across the Atlantic in horrifying conditions in the notorious 'middle passage' and sold in the Americas; the ships were then filled with sugar, tobacco, mahogany or raw cotton for the third leg back to England. They expected to turn a profit on each stage of the journey and huge fortunes were made, in particular in Bristol and Liverpool. However, by 1800 Liverpool had manifestly overtaken its southern rival and was extending its lead. Bristol still had a vigorous community of merchants and industrialists, though, and in the 1820s they were looking for ways to restore their city's commercial position: it was this group who were to give Isambard his greatest professional opportunities.

It may be that what drew him to their city in the first place was the competition for the Clifton Bridge. Bristol stands on the north side of the Avon, about five miles upriver from the open sea. Between the city and the sea, the river passes through a short but deep limestone gorge, and this had long formed an obstacle to Bristol's communications. In 1753 an alderman of the city, William Vick, died leaving £1,000 in trust to Bristol's

Society of Merchant Venturers, specifying that when it had grown by compound interest to £10,000 it was to be used to build a stone bridge across the Avon gorge, for it seems that some wild optimist had told him that the gorge could indeed be bridged for this sum. In 1829 the Vick legacy had grown to £8,000 and the Merchant Venturers had grown tired of waiting. A committee was appointed, but swiftly established that a stone bridge of such huge size (for the gorge is over 600 feet wide and 200 feet deep) would cost something more like £90,000. So the Merchant Venturers advertised a competition for a suspension bridge, believing that this would be substantially cheaper, and by their closing date in November 1829 22 plans had been sent in, including four by Isambard Kingdom Brunel.

That Isambard should have sent in four different designs reflects his fertility as a designer, his energy, and maybe the fact that he had time on his hands since the Thames Tunnel had ground to a halt. They were for different sites within the zone specified by the committee, with spans ranging from 760 feet to 1,180 feet: it should be borne in mind that his father's suspension bridges on the Île de Bourbon had spans of 131 feet 9 inches, and the widest span in existence, only completed in 1826, was Telford's Menai Bridge with a clear span of 600 feet. So even his most modest design would have been, by some margin, the longest suspension bridge in the world. His designs bristled with novel features: the suspension chains would have links 15 feet long, twice the size of the Menai Bridge's links, which would be pinned directly to each other through their end lugs. The deck would have equalising beams, to ensure that the chains were carrying the same load, and a system of transverse bracing, to stiffen it against wind action. Brunel's plans, and those of four other competitors, were shortlisted, and submitted to the consideration of Thomas Telford, the undoubted doyen of bridge builders.

Unfortunately, Telford declared that his Menai Bridge represented the greatest span that could safely be achieved: this may have been professional pride speaking, but probably also had something to do with his concerns about the bridge's behaviour in high winds. Mr Brunel's designs, he announced, were unsafe, and for good measure he rejected all the other candidates as well. The committee took the hint and asked Telford if he would design them a bridge himself.

At this point, Isambard seems to have given up on Bristol. He went to 'smoke away his anger' in a tour of northern England, and applied unsuccessfully for the post of engineer to the Newcastle & Carlisle Railway. 1830 was the lowest point of his whole career: he got one proper job, draining Tollesbury Marshes in Essex. In November, thanks to an introduction from Charles Babbage, he seemed to be in with a chance of being appointed as engineer to the Birmingham & Bristol Railway, but this too evaporated. There was one other cause for celebration: in June 1830 at the age of 24, he was elected to the Royal Society.

Meanwhile, Telford had produced a rather strange-looking design for a bridge at Clifton, with a central span 360 feet wide made possible by the construction of enormous Gothic towers rising from the bottom of the gorge. The people of Bristol did not like the look of it: in January 1831 they held another competition and Isambard entered another design, with a good deal of help from his father. Telford's scheme was set aside on the grounds of the cost of the huge towers, and on 18 March Brunel was declared to be the winner. Sensing the committee's caution, he had reduced his span to 630 feet, about as small as it could be while still clearing the whole gorge in one leap, though this would involve constructing a massive abutment on the south side. It was still the longest span that anyone had seriously contemplated building, and its suspension chains and deck would be novel in design, along the same lines as his previous schemes. Finally, the towers would be Egyptian in style, clad in cast-iron panels, with relief sculptures depicting all the processes that went into manufacturing and building the bridge. The Bristolians were captivated, and a foundation stone was laid on the Leigh Woods side on 27 August 1831. However, it turned out to be a false start: work stopped immediately and was not resumed until 1836.

Isambard took up periodic residence in Clifton in 1831: in October, when the city erupted in riots, he enlisted as a special constable and arrested a man. He was making useful contacts in the city, but actual work continued to be elusive, and in November he set off again for another tour of the North. The dock company at Monkwearmouth wanted to build new harbour facilities, on the north side of the Wear estuary, near Sunderland. He was appointed as their engineer, but received no payment for his trouble and expense in travelling north, and the work took a long time to get going. He travelled south again, admiring Durham Cathedral, but gazing rather contemptuously at the Scotswood Viaduct on the Stockton & Darlington Railway, a suspension bridge which deflected by about a foot each time a train went across it (it didn't last in use very much longer). Passing through Manchester in December, he took his first railway journey, on the year-old Liverpool & Manchester line.

1832 must have been almost as frustrating as the two previous years: his designs for Monkwearmouth Dock were rejected by Parliament, and the Gaz Engine was clearly going nowhere. On 30 January 1833 he wrote:

Gaz – after a number of experiments I fear we must come to the conclusion that (with carbonic acid at least) no sufficient advantages on the score of economy of fuel can be obtained. All the time and expense, both enormous, devoted to this thing for nearly 10 years are therefore wasted . . . It must therefore die and with it all my fine hopes – crash – gone – well, well, it can't be helped.

One bright point of the year was his meeting his future wife, Mary Horsley, and her family.

At length, Bristol provided another professional opportunity. Bristol's docks, eight miles up the Avon, had always had problems owing to the river's restricted size, high tidal range, and its tendency to silt up, and in 1803–9 the canal engineer William Jessop had been called in. His solution was bracingly radical: a straight new waterway, the 'New Cut', was dug to take the flow of the river, while the original course of the Avon as it meandered through the city was dammed to retain water at a consistent level: this became known as the 'Floating Harbour'. Jessop also dug the 'Feeder Canal' to boost the water supply. Given the constraints of the geography it was a brilliant solution which gave Bristol's docks another century of vigorous use, but they still couldn't compete with Liverpool's huge and expanding capacity, and the Floating Harbour displayed a continuing tendency to silt up. Isambard was asked to investigate. His first report, presented on 31 August 1832, diagnosed the basic problem as insufficient flow of water and prescribed a number of solutions. They should raise the weir to raise the water level, introduce regular dredging, and widen the entrance locks. The Dock Company, an increasingly torpid institution, commissioned him to carry out a modest first round of works: alterations to the Rownham Dam, and a new drag boat. Isambard produced a second report for them in 1842. Gradually, with support from the more energetic elements, he was allowed to carry out some further works: raising the Netham Dam, rebuilding the South Entrance Lock, installing a remarkable swing bridge at the Cumberland Basin entrance, and introducing a second drag boat (so serviceable that it was operating into the 1960s).

The problem was that the Floating Harbour, for all Jessop's ingenuity and Isambard's improvements, was simply too small to allow Bristol to compete. The tension between Isambard and the reactionary elements in the Dock Company increased, when his first two ships, the *Great Western* and the *Great Britain*, both turned out to be too large to operate out of the Floating Harbour. He pressed the Dock Company to build new ocean-going facilities on the Severn at Avonmouth, but got nowhere. A second proposal, for a deep-water pier at Portbury, led to the establishment of a Portbury Pier and Railway Company in 1846, but work stopped again in 1852.

What was stopping them? The answer, in part, seems to have been that the Dock Company was dominated by vested interests, who owned property on the Floating Harbour and did not want to see it devalued. More generally, Bristol's spirit of enterprise seemed to be flagging, as the city fell further and further behind its northern rival. Nevertheless, Bristol's commercial decline remains hard to understand, for it still had citizens who were both rich and energetic, and who were to give Isambard his greatest opportunities, as railway engineer and ship designer.

For one thing, work had started on the Clifton Bridge for real, with a second foundation laying on 27 August 1836. To help transfer materials from one side to the other, a wrought-iron rod 1 inch in diameter and 1,000 feet long was made, and pulled into position spanning the gorge, and a travelling basket hung from it, pulled by ropes. On the first day, the bar kinked, the basket stuck there and its ropes became entangled with a ship passing below: Isambard insisted that he should be in the basket which made the next run, and when, perhaps predictably, it got stuck in the middle, he swung up to the bar, to free it, high above the

A vivid drawing of the construction of the Euston Extension of the London & Birmingham Railway by George Scharf c. 1837.

One of Brunel's designs for the Clifton Bridge, from the spring of 1831. The towers were to be styled like the gateways of an Egyptian temple.

A 'Firefly' class locomotive emerges from the 'Number 1 Tunnel' in between Bath and Bristol. This was the title-page image of John Cooke Bourne's superbly illustrated *History of the Great Western Railway*, published in 1846.

An anonymous portrait of Sophia Brunel, Marc's wife.

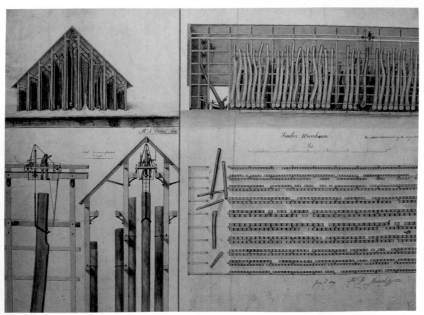

A 'timber warehouse' probably intended for the Royal Naval Dockyard at Chatham, though it is not known to have been built. Note the travelling gantry with its hydraulic lifting equipment.

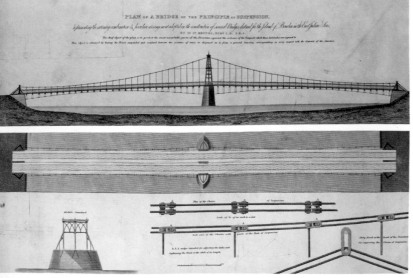

Marc Brunel's design for one of two suspension bridges commissioned by the French government and built on the Île de Bourbon in the Indian Ocean. The ironwork was manufactured in Sheffield, and Isambard had to make several journeys to supervise the work before it was finally shipped out in November 1823.

A coloured lithograph of 1836 showing the Thames Tunnel as Marc Brunel had envisaged it, with stairs for pedestrians down one of the access shafts, all decorated in crisp Neoclassical style.

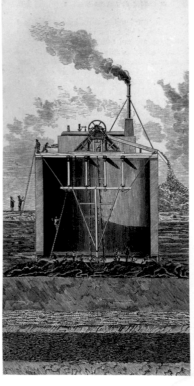

A cross-section of the Rotherhithe shaft being sunk. Workmen removed the earth from within the tower and loaded it onto the bucket chain, powered by the steam engine on top. As the earth was removed, the iron cutting edge at the foot of the tower cut into the ground and the whole structure sank.

An oil painting by an anonymous artist of the banquet that the Brunels held in the tunnel on 10 November 1827.

The most ambitious of Brunel's four designs for the Clifton Bridge envisaged a clear span of 1,180 feet, almost twice that of Telford's Menai Bridge. The approach roads would be tunnelled through the rock, and the chains would be suspended between turrets rising directly from the top of the cliffs.

August 1836 and work begins on the Clifton Bridge with the slinging of a 1,000-foot-long wrought-iron rod across the gorge to carry materials.

Isambard Kingdom Brunel, portrayed in 1835 by his brother-in-law John Calcott Horsley, with a copy of the parliamentary survey for the Great Western Railway.

Sir Marc Isambard Brunel by Samuel Drummond, showing the Thames Tunnel in the background.

The Great Western Railway line as submitted with the company's second and successful parliamentary bill in 1835. It shows the GWR linking up with the London & Birmingham Railway at a proposed joint terminus at Euston. This was later rejected in favour of a new station at Paddington.

J.C. Bourne's beautiful lithograph of the Wharncliffe Viaduct from the *History of the Great Western Railway* which follows the route of the railway from London to Bristol. Bourne emphasises the contrast between the noble grandeur of the viaduct, with its Egyptian-influenced piers, and the rustic scenes around it.

A view of the main engine house at Swindon, where Gooch established the GWR's 'principal locomotive establishment'. Note the elegant timber roof trusses tied with wrought-iron rods, and the long 'traverser' that the locomotive is sitting on.

J.C. Bourne's beautiful coloured view gives an idea of the great height of Box Hill, rising behind: note the first-generation signal and its attendant 'policeman', or in later terms, signalman.

chasm. It was a very public display of physical courage, not unmixed with self-advertisement.

The cliffs were made safe, the foundations were cut, and the great towers rose very slowly from 1836, delayed by the bankruptcy of the main contractor. At last, Brunel was allowed to place an order for the suspension chains: 1,150 links were made at the Copperhouse Foundry at Hayle in Cornwall. However, they were never to be hung at Clifton. In 1843 the bridge company became insolvent and work stopped. The chains were eventually sold to build another of Isambard's masterpieces, the Royal Albert Bridge at Saltash, but the towers above the Clifton gorge still stood, abandoned, at the time of his death. It was a frustrating end for the project which he had referred to in 1835 as 'my first child, my darling'.

By this time, though, his career had taken off decisively, again, thanks to Bristol. The city needed a railway, to help defend its declining share of the Atlantic trade. Liverpool's merchants and bankers had been among the main supporters of canal development, and now they were in the lead in financing the first railways. Bristol was connected to its markets and hinterlands at home by a few winding roads and canals. Liverpool, on the other hand, after 1830, was connected to its main hinterland by the Liverpool & Manchester Railway, the fastest and most revolutionary transport system in the world. What was more, Liverpudlian money was already behind schemes to build railways southwards, to Birmingham and London (one of the many remarkable points about all this is how little of the initiative for the first railways actually came from London). If Bristol was to stay in the game, they too needed a railway linking them to London. In fact, the city produced five or six failed attempts to set up a railway company between 1824 and 1832: the sheer scale of the project was unprecedented and it was almost impossible to say what it would cost – a difficult point for any commercial venture.

In the autumn of 1832 four of the city's merchants assembled to make another attempt to establish a 'Bristol Railway'. This time the venture took off: the City's Corporation, Dock Company, Chamber of Commerce and Society of Merchant Venturers came on board. A public meeting was held in January 1833, funds were raised to pay for a survey and in February they began to look for an engineer. There were a number of local candidates in the picture, notably William Brunton and Henry Price, who were already canvassing support for their own scheme, and William Townshend, the surveyor to the Bristol & Gloucestershire Railway (an ambitiously titled coal tramway), but Isambard's name was well known in Bristol by this time and he had influential supporters. He travelled from London to Bristol on the overnight mail coach (sitting on the outside, to save money) on 6 March 1833, to hear the committee's verdict. At 2 p.m. on the 7th he heard that he had been appointed, by a majority of one. The proviso was that he should work with William Townshend for the sake of the latter's local knowledge. On 9 March, Isambard set out with Townshend up the Avon valley on horseback, to begin their survey. He was 27 years old. It was the greatest opportunity – indeed it was the turning point – of his whole career.

3

From the collapse of the Thames Tunnel in January 1828 until 1833 Isambard was obliged to lead a fairly peripatetic life. He took lodgings in Brighton, then in Clifton, and travelled widely in search of work, but the nearest thing he had to a fixed abode was his sister Sophia Hawes's house, Barge House in Lambeth, or his parents' establishment in Blackfriars. These were frustrating years for Marc and Sophia: Marc wrangled fruitlessly with the Tunnel Company directors and lobbied Parliament for the funds to rescue and complete his vision. The rest of his practice had largely fallen away. Isambard was now working independently, and the Clifton Bridge competition marked a subtle shift in their relationship, with Marc occasionally assisting his son, rather than vice versa.

Isambard's appointment to carry out the GWR's survey was followed, in August 1833, by his appointment as their engineer at a salary of £2,000. It was the turning point in his career, and the first time that he had had significant means of his own. He also needed to set up an office and staff very quickly, and in July he leased 53 Parliament Street, just north of the Palace of Westminster in an area already favoured by the engineering profession. It was a substantial terraced house, as large as anything his parents had ever had. He established his household there and also his office, which for the time being he shared with his father.

Isambard had had a number of romantic attachments from his teenage years. The most important seems to have been to a girl called Ellen Hulme, a member of a family the Brunels knew in Manchester. It is not clear how he first met her: they evidently corresponded over some years in the late 1820s, and although none of these letters seem to survive, several entries in his private diary give insights into his feelings for her, his fears for the future, and his grand imaginings, of which two passages must suffice here:

19 October 1827
Q. Shall I make a good husband? Am doubtful. My ambition or whatever it may be called (it is not the mere wish to be rich) is rather extensive but still I am not afraid that I shall be unhappy if I do not reach the rank of Hero and Commander-in-Chief of His Majesty's Forces in the steam (or Gaz) boat department. This is a favourite 'Castle in the Air' of mine. Make the Gaz engine answer, fit out some vessels (of course a war), take some prizes, nay, some fortified town, get employed by Government contract and command a fine fleet and fight – fight – in fact take Algiers or something in that style. Build a splendid manufactory for Gaz engines, a

yard for building the boats – and at last be rich, have a house built of which I have even made the drawings. Be the first Engineer and example for all future ones.

And on 27 November 1827

> I have had, as I suppose most young men have had, numerous attachments, if they deserve the name. Each in its turn has appeared to me the true one. E.H. is the oldest and most constant, now however gone by. During her reign, nearly 7 years, several inferior ones caught my attention, I need only remind myself of Mme D.C., O.S., and numerous others. With E. Hume (sic) it was mutual. The sofa scenes must now appear to her, as to me, rather ridiculous . . . [and after a missing section of the diary, evidently cut out] . . . served me right if I had been spilled in the mud – certainly a devilish pretty girl, an excellent musician and a very sweet voice – but I'm afraid those eyes don't speak of a very placid temper.

By 1830 the attachment to Ellen seems to have been over, though not forgotten: there is some evidence that she never married, and that right through the 1840s Brunel was paying an annuity to her and her sister.

In 1832 he was introduced to the Horsley family of Kensington, probably by his brother-in-law Benjamin Hawes. William Horsley was an organist, teacher and composer, married to Elizabeth Calcott, daughter of another composer and niece to a well-known painter. They had four children: John became a notable artist and was a lifelong friend to Isambard; Fanny was a fine amateur painter; Sophy was a talented amateur musician; and Mary, aged 19 in 1832, was the family beauty. They were a singularly cultivated family, in a way that hardly exists any more and to a degree which must have been rare even at the time.

They numbered many artists and musicians among their friends: Mendelssohn was a frequent guest on his visits to London. Life at 1 High Row, Kensington Gravel Pits was marked by family concerts, impromptu musical sessions around the piano, and plays and charades, many of them of their own devising.

Isambard's appointment as the GWR's engineer in 1833 gave him a regular income for the first time. While this meant that, financially speaking, he could contemplate marriage, the pressure of work involved probably served to delay this step for almost three years. When he could spare the time, though, he continued to visit at 1 High Row, joining in with the family concerts and theatricals. At length, towards the end of 1835, with work about to begin on the London end of the railway, he made up his mind, and on an evening in May 1836 he proposed to Mary on a family walk. They were married at Kensington on 5 July and went for two weeks' honeymoon in North Wales. They returned to London and set up house at 18 Duke Street, overlooking St James's Park, a couple of hundred yards from Parliament Street.

In fact, Isambard had already leased and moved into Duke Street in December 1835. This in itself suggests that he was already moving towards a decision about marriage, for it would have been a very grand establishment for a bachelor: the previous occupant had been the Earl of Devon. It was a large, early 18th-century house of red brick, four storeys high, looking rather like the houses which still exist on nearby Queen Anne's Gate. The house was entered from Duke Street on an upper ground floor, below which was a lower ground floor at the level of the park. His office seems to have occupied part of these lower floors, but after a while he put up a detached building measuring 40 feet by 20 in the garden, to house his draughtsmen and clerks: rather characteristically, it was covered with a flat roof terrace of pioneering construction, made of tiles set in cement and carried on iron beams. While her husband worked downstairs, Mary presided in her drawing room on the first floor: it was to be their home for the rest of their lives.

Mary's personality is rather elusive. In her teens, her family had nicknamed her the 'Duchess of Kensington' for a certain hauteur of manner, though her granddaughter Lady Noble testified to her underlying warmth of nature. The one thing we know for certain is that she was universally regarded as a beauty, and comported herself as such. She was presented at court by her sister-in-law Lady Hawes, so magnificently dressed that her niece, Maria Hawes complained:

> The Queen never took her eyes off Aunt Mary, but followed her to the end of the room, and I had no chance of being noticed, coming behind her immense crinoline.

No letters from her seem to survive, and very few from Isambard to her. One rare exception, written while he was working on the GWR's main line around Wootton Bassett in 1840, gives us a certain insight into their relationship:

> *My Dearest Mary,*
> I have become quite a walker. I have walked today from Bathford Bridge to here – all but about one mile, which makes eighteen miles walking along the line – and I really am not very tired. I am, however, going to sleep here – if I had been half an hour earlier, I think I could not have withstood the temptation of coming up by the six ½ train, and returning by the morning goods train, just to see you; however, I will write you a long letter instead. It is a blowy evening, pouring with rain, my last two miles were wet. I arrived of course rather wet, and found the hotel, which is the best of a set of deplorable public houses, full – and here

I am at the 'Cow and Candlesnuffers' or some such sign – a large room or cave, for it seems open to the wind everywhere, old-fashioned, with a large chimney in one corner; but unfortunately it has one of these horrible little stoves, just nine inches across [a sketch of a tiny grate]. I have piled a fire upon both hobs, but to little use, there are four doors and two windows. What's the use of the doors I can't conceive, for you might crawl under them if they happened to be locked, and they seem too crooked to open, the ones with not a bad bit of looking glass between them, seem particularly friendlily disposed [here, he drew a cartoon of the doors leaning drunkenly inwards, to either side of a handsome Georgian mirror].

The window curtains very wisely are not drawn, as they would be blown right across the room and probably over the two extra greasy muttons [candles] which are on the table, giving just light enough to see the results of their evident attempts to outvie each other trying which can make the better snuff. One of them is quite a splendid fellow, a sort of black colliflower, and I don't like to destroy him, so I send you a picture of him [a cartoon of an especially smoky-looking candle] . . .

I hope this very interesting letter will reach you safely, dearest . . .

. . . There is a horrible harp, upon which really and truly somebody has every few minutes for the last three hours been strumming these chords always the same.

Good-bye my dearest Love,

Yours,

I.K. Brunel

Ever since the Thames Tunnel collapse in January 1828, Isambard's father had been struggling to save and finish his unachieved vision. £193,000 had been subscribed, of which £180,000 had been spent, and Marc estimated that completing it would cost another £200,000. Years went by in apparently fruitless lobbying: Marc used the time in helping his son on the Clifton Bridge designs, then later, on some of the early stages of work on the Great Western Railway. All his years of work on the tunnel seemed to have been for nothing, but he never became embittered. In February 1829, a young English traveller, Charles MacFarlane, chanced to meet Isambard while travelling from Paris back to London and, once back in town, was introduced to the Brunel parents. He left a vivid account of visiting the house in Blackfriars and ascending to the drawing room:

> where I found his mother, a very charming, unaffected, warm-hearted, thorough English gentlewoman, who received me as if she had known me all my life. I returned the five sovereigns, at which she laughed rather heartily, as she did also at some of the stories about our journey . . .
>
> Best of all, I met the head of the house, dear old Brunel, to whom, in an instant, I flew and attached myself as a needle to a big lode-stone. Not that old Isambard was big, on the contrary, he was a rather smaller man than his son. The dear old man had – with a great deal more warmth of heart than belonged to that school – the manner, bearing, address, and even dress, of a French gentleman of the ancien regime, for he had kept to a rather antiquated, but very becoming costume.
>
> I was perfectly charmed with him at this our first meeting, and from many subsequent ones I can feel bold enough to say that he was a man of the kindest and most simple heart, and of the acutest and purest taste . . . And what I most admired of all, was his thorough simplicity and unworldliness of character, his indifference to mere lucre, and his genuine

absent-mindedness . . . He had lived as if there were no rogues in this nether world.

These qualities had to sustain Marc through another five years and more of waiting and lobbying. At length, in July 1834, a Treasury loan of £270,000 to the Thames Tunnel Company was approved, but even after this it took another year for the funds to be released, and for them to resume work: Marc was then 66 years old. Isambard was no longer available, having been claimed by the Great Western Railway, so Marc re-engaged Richard Beamish, the ex-guardsman. A new and better tunnelling shield was commissioned and constructed: it took a long time to install, and it wasn't until March 1836 that they were ready to move again. Work had been delayed for eight years. The tunnel crept forward: the work was as foul and dangerous as before, and the Thames burst in three more times before the miners reached the north shore. In the spring of 1841, work started on the Wapping shaft, conceived as a 'sinking tower' in the same way as the Rotherhithe shaft. By the autumn the shaft was finished and in November the first contact was made. At last, on 10 January 1842, the sections of the Shield were lined up at the bottom of the Wapping shaft, their job done. Marc's lifetime of labour had already received the recognition it deserved: on 24 March 1841 he had been knighted by Queen Victoria.

With the tunnel complete, Marc and Sophia moved from Rotherhithe to a house on Park Street, not far from their son's residence on Duke Street. There they spent a peaceful old age, taking holidays in Devon via Isambard's Great Western Railway, and taking an interest in their grandchildren. This seems to have been marred only by occasional tensions with their daughter-in-law, Mary. A friend, Mrs Crosland, left us this evocation of the elderly couple:

I believe I was a good listener, and assured of my sympathy they poured out their reminiscences freely, or rather, I should say, Lady Brunel did, for the old man was not voluble, though he often by a nod of the head or some short exclamation confirmed his wife's words. She was a little old lady, with her faculties bright and apparently unimpaired; he with a ponderous head surmounting what might be called a thick-set figure. The old couple usually sat side by side and often the old man would take his wife's withered hand in his, sometimes raising it to his lips with the restrained fervour of a respectful lover.

Sir Marc died on 12 December 1849, aged 80, and was buried in Kensal Green cemetery. Sophia went to live with her son and his family at 18 Duke Street, and lived on until January 1855.

Duke Street had just become a larger and grander establishment, for in 1848 Isambard had bought the lease to number 17, the neighbouring house to the north. Substantial alterations seem to have been made: doorways were formed between the two houses and they were run as a single establishment. Both houses seem to have had a lower ground floor which looked out over St James's Park, and an upper ground floor at the level of Duke Street. After 1848 the lower floors of number 18 seem to have been occupied by the Brunels' domestic staff, with the kitchen, the butler's pantry and servants' hall: the office seems to have moved into the lower floors of number 17. Isambard himself occupied a large room on the ground floor, overlooking the park.

His growing wealth was reflected in the lavish decoration and furnishings of the house. An inventory of the contents was made in 1858, when the financial problems arising from the *Great Eastern*, in which he had a large shareholding, were looking particularly pressing. Number 18, evidently the larger house, had the drawing room and 'Organ Room', named for the chamber organ which was the focus of family concerts. The drawing room was decorated with paintings by Mary's family: two by her brother John, and no less than seventeen by her great-uncle, Augustus Calcott. The contents of the Larder included a 'best dinner service' of Berlin ware, and a 'best tea service' of Dresden china, while the butler's pantry housed £2,886-worth of plate. The Brunels created one major set piece of interior design: a new dining room in number 17: it was very much a period piece in the taste of the time, with an elaborate plastered ceiling with pendants in the Elizabethan style, a chimneypiece with marble figures worth £185, a 'richly carved sideboard' worth £300, a Venetian glass chandelier and mirrors, and hangings and curtains of crimson silk. A series of specially commissioned paintings depicting scenes from Shakespeare's plays continued the Elizabethan theme: ten paintings were commissioned and hung (though apparently more were intended), by artists including John Horsley, and such well-known Academicians as Edwin Landseer and Clarkson Stanfield. Isambard added to his collections on his travels abroad, especially on two journeys with his brother-in-law Horsley, to Paris in 1849, and to Italy in 1852, buying pictures, bronzes and fine French furniture. His parents could never have afforded such splendour.

It was a substantial household: the 1851 census recorded that 17 individuals were living there. The immediate family then consisted of Isambard and Mary Brunel, aged 44 and 37, the widowed 76-year-old Lady Brunel, and the three children, Isambard aged 13, Henry Marc aged 8 and Florence aged 3. There was a governess and two nurses (whether for the children or for Lady Brunel is not clear), a butler, a housekeeper, a cook, a lady's maid for Mary, three housemaids and a kitchen maid.

Isambard worked very long hours and was often away at his

business, but nevertheless, such evidence as we have suggests that he was a fond and affectionate father: family servants testified to how he would hurry upstairs from his office to the nursery to see them, occasionally entertaining them with kite flying and conjuring tricks. On one occasion in 1843 he was performing conjuring tricks for a party of children at his house, including one which involved him appearing to swallow a sovereign and produce it from out of his ear: unfortunately, he really did swallow it, and it lodged in his trachea and remained there for some weeks, potentially endangering his life. Isambard himself devised a means whereby he was strapped to a board which was rotated until the coin, shaken loose, fell out of his mouth again. The accident, and its aftermath, caused a great stir.

Certainly, Brunel's children all remained deeply devoted to his memory after his death. Nevertheless he could be stern, according to the fashion of his age. Isambard Junior, his eldest son, developed a shuffling gait from a slight deformity in one leg at an early age: this might have been corrected by surgery, but for his mother's opposition to the idea. His father, too, seems to have adopted a bracingly Victorian approach to this disability:

if I could have you under my care for three months, I feel sure I could cure you. I wish I could do it, my dear fellow, but you must try and do it for yourself.

A similar spirit seems to pervade another letter to Mary in April 1844, when Isambard Junior had just been sent away to Harrow:

. . . I hope, dearest, you are well and happy. You are wrong in supposing that I cannot feel your parting with dear Isambard. I hope the poor little fellow is not very unhappy, but it is what all must go through, and he has infinitely less cause for pain than most boys in beginning. I made my beginning in ten times worse circumstances, and now he will soon get over it. Give my love to the dear boy, and tell him I have smoked his cigar case twice empty.

Adieu, dearest, love to Baby,

Yours devotedly,

I.K. Brunel.

A warmer and probably fairer view of Brunel as a parent may be gained from another letter to Isambard Junior on his 18th birthday, in 1855:

May 20th 1855.

My dear Isambard,

You are now eighteen, getting into manhood, and I, of course, going down the other side of the hill.

May you have as much happiness as I, your father, have had; and try and remember always that at least half the evils of life – and those by far the most difficult to bear – are of one's own creation, either by follies and imprudences, or by obstinate and wilful omission.

And, my dear Isambard, although my constant engagements have prevented my seeing so much of my children as I should have wished, yet I hope that you would look upon me as your first friend to consult, if ever you got into difficulties or had any doubt as to your proper course . . .

Pray then, my dear boy, while you have a Father, to whom you might safely and without annoyance to yourself, confide anything, consult him if you ever have the slightest difficulty; and to you, my dear Isambard, many happy returns of the day.

Your affectionate father,

I.K. Brunel.

Over the first line of the fourth sentence, his son later wrote 'Alas! Alas!'– a sad comment on his father's early death.

Isambard Junior grew up delicate and bookish, and before long it became clear that he had little interest in his father's profession. The second son, Henry Marc, however, showed every sign of interest: his father taught him mathematics and the fundamentals of engineering, and in the later 1850s began occasionally to take Henry on business trips; in 1858 the boy was released from Harrow at his father's request, to witness the launch of the *Great Eastern*.

From the early 1840s, Isambard used to take his family on annual summer holidays, usually to the West Country. He began to look around for a property to buy, and in 1847, while staying in Torquay, he found the right place. It was a substantial piece of land at Watcombe, overlooking Babbacombe Bay. There was no house on the property, but from that point the Brunels would rent a house in the neighbourhood for their annual holiday. The land was a series of fields, but he began landscaping and terracing it, and planting trees to create fine grounds, with the help of the celebrated garden designer William Eden Nesfield. In spare moments, he also made sketches of the country house that he planned to build there: his sketchbooks have a number of drawings for a villa in an Italian style. Brunel built a small chapel for the use of his staff at Watcombe and, in 1851, he gave them all a week's holiday, to go and see the Great Exhibition in Hyde Park. At some point, probably in 1854, Brunel changed his mind and commissioned designs for a substantial country house in a French chateau style, from the eminent architect William Burn: full designs for this were made, but he was never to build his dream house. From 1853 he was heavily involved in the construction of the *Great Eastern* and, as with all his projects, he invested heavily in it. The cost, in both time and money, put paid to the plans for a house at Watcombe, and when Isambard died in 1859 the broad terrace with the wonderful sea view that he had created there was still empty.

Brunel travelled abroad on a number of occasions: to Italy with John Horsley in 1842; to Italy again, about the Genoa Railway, in 1845; to Switzerland with Mary in 1846; to Paris with Horsley soon after the Revolution in 1848; and to the Continent again with Mary and Isambard in 1852. Thereafter, the *Great Eastern* consumed ever more of his time, money and energy, and he only made one more foreign trip, in the winter of 1858–9, and that was at his doctors' orders, for by then he was seriously ill.

All the published biographies of Brunel have tended to assume that his death at the age of 53 was brought on by the stress and overwork caused by the building of the *Great Eastern*. There is only very limited evidence to go on, but it is worth questioning this assumption. Certainly by any normal standards he had been over-taxing himself for many years, but there is little or no evidence up to 1857 that this had made all that much difference. He suffered serious injuries in the Thames Tunnel in 1828 and in a fall on board the *Great Western* in 1838, but seems to have made a fairly good recovery from both of these events. He had an encouraging genetic inheritance: his father Marc also worked immensely hard for most of his adult life, and both he and Sophia lived to be 80. The famous photographs of Brunel taken by Robert Howlett at the failed launch of the *Great Eastern* in November 1857, taken at the moment when the strain must have been at its peak, do not look like images of a sick man. In the summer of 1858, though, he was diagnosed by Richard Bright and Sir Benjamin Brodie as suffering from a condition of the kidneys, first identified by the first of these eminent physicians and originally named Bright's Disease.

Bright's Disease is now known as glomerulonephritis: its pathology is not fully understood today, but essentially it is characterised by inflammation of the microscopic filters in the kidneys, leading to renal failure. There are a number of possible causes, among which the main ones seem to be a form of bacterial infection, and an adverse reaction to this by the immune system. Alternatively, Brunel's years of heavy cigar smoking may have raised his blood pressure, and this would have put his kidneys (as well as his heart) under strain. As the condition worsened, and the levels of waste products built up in his bloodstream, he would have suffered from anaemia, raised blood pressure and exhaustion. His doctors were probably the best in the world, and the diagnosis would have been the most accurate available. Today the disease would be treated by dialysis or a transplant: then, there was no treatment, and the best that Dr Bright could advise was rest and a warm climate.

So Brunel left, with Mary, Henry, a junior doctor and several servants, for an extended tour of Italy and Egypt. Many of the passengers were seasick on the boat from Marseilles, but Brunel, unable to cease from his observations, remained on the deck huddled against the paddle box, making notes of the behaviour of the ship. Then travelling up the Nile to Aswan and back, the Brunel family returned to England via Italy, spending Easter in Rome. On his return to England, it soon became clear that he was not really any better, and as the *Great Eastern* neared completion in the summer of 1859, his condition worsened. Brunel was on board the great ship on 5 September 1859, the day before it was due to sail for its first sea-trials when, in his son's words, he 'felt symptoms of failing power' and had to be taken home. The attack is also described as 'paralysis': maybe this was a heart-related event, caused by the high blood pressure. At any rate he did not recover, though he seems to have remained conscious till the end, and died on 15 September.

4

Railways

Today, we rather take railways for granted, noticing them most when they go wrong. They seem like part of the landscape, and it requires an effort of imagination to grasp what a vast cultural and economic achievement they represented when they were new, and what they meant to the people who built them.

The railways evolved out of a number of ideas and technologies which had developed over the previous 50 years and more in Georgian Britain. First, a demand for better inland communications had led to hundreds of turnpike trusts being set up by town councils or by groups of the county gentry, to build new tollroads. Then mail-coach services, often of remarkable sophistication and regularity, were developed to run over the new roads. Then, from the 1760s on, thousands of miles of canals were dug, providing the country with a new bulk-transport system for goods. Building the roads and canals required very accurate surveying and map making. They also involved gargantuan feats of earth moving, all done by hand. Cheap labour was readily available, for the population was rising, and huge numbers of poor country-dwellers were being thrown off the land by agricultural reform. Whatever its image as an 'age of elegance', this was a harsh, unsentimental society.

Mining engineers had long noticed that it was much easier to move bulk goods like coal or stone in waggons running on rails, than on an ordinary road surface: by 1800 several hundred mines and quarries were using horse-drawn tramways. The same mines often used stationary steam engines to pump water or drive machinery. So, in the early 1800s the first steam locomotives were invented and built to run on tramways at ironworks and collieries, such as the Penydarren locomotive in 1804, and George Stephenson's 'Blucher' in 1814. Once viable locomotives had been developed events moved remarkably quickly, thanks to the initiative of a tiny number of mostly northern engineers, businessmen and financiers. They opened the Stockton & Darlington Railway in 1824, the Canterbury & Whitstable Railway in 1825 and, much the most important, the Liverpool & Manchester Railway in 1830.

All of this was done by private initiative and money:

Georgian Britain was the ultimate free-enterprise society. Where the state did have a role was in providing a legal framework through Acts of Parliament. Property was regarded as sacrosanct, but they knew that, to develop trade, they needed better roads and new canals, which would inevitably interfere with property rights. So during the 18th century a practice developed whereby a turnpike trust or a canal company secured official authorisation by Act of Parliament. This was partly an acknowledgement that a turnpike trust or a canal company, by nature, tended to be a monopoly provider, and that some kind of higher authorisation was needed for this. An Act of Parliament gave the new company authority to levy tolls, to raise share capital, and to enter and purchase property compulsorily. Not surprisingly, the business of securing an Act of Parliament for a road or a canal was often attended by fierce controversy and lobbying, at both local and national level.

So when railways were first planned these ideas and assumptions – that they would be built and run by private companies; that they would raise money by selling shares; that they would need parliamentary authorisation; and that they would be vigorously promoted by one set of local interests and vehemently opposed by others – were fully formed, having been developed in the 'canal mania' of the previous fifty years. The difference, and what sharpened the whole situation, was that the new railways would obviously be in direct competition with the mail coaches and the canal companies, many of which were not all that old, and many of which would indeed be put out of business.

All of this would have been in the background and part of Brunel's mental furniture when he rode out of Bristol with William Townshend on 9 March 1833, to begin his survey for the new 'Bristol Railway'. He was setting out to find the route for the longest railway that had yet been envisaged (118 miles, as

against 114 miles for the contemporary London & Birmingham
Railway). He had no experience of designing such a thing, but
then, very few people had. Indeed, Brunel's entire experience of
railways seems to have been that he had had a look at the
Stockton & Darlington, and taken one return trip on the
Liverpool & Manchester, on his journey north in the winter of
1831. He had written in his notebook:

> I record this specimen of the shaking on the Manchester
> Railway. The time is not far off when we shall be able to take
> our coffee and write while going noiselessly and smoothly at
> 45 mph. Let me try.

The remark says a good deal for Brunel's self-confidence,
especially when one reflects that, up to 1830, no one in history
had ever travelled at anything like that speed.

Certain principles governing railway design had already been
established, the most important being that the line needs to be
as level and as straight as possible. From the outset Brunel was
planning his railway as an integrated system, 'the best of all
possible railways', designed for smooth running and high speed.
Two other Bristol surveyors, Brunton and Price, had been
promoting a rival scheme for a 'southerly' route, going from Bath
up the Avon valley via Trowbridge, Devizes and Hungerford,
joining the Thames valley at Reading. This would indeed have
delivered the traffic of those towns, but at the cost of a winding
route with steep gradients, slowing everything down. Brunel
grasped from the outset that this represented a fundamental
error: the essence of a national railway network was that it
should have fast 'trunk routes' linking the main centres. The
branch lines, picking up the smaller towns and remoter regions,
could come later, and it wouldn't really matter if they were
rather slower. So he opted for a 'northern' route, which ran from

London up the Thames valley to Reading, but from there headed north via Didcot and Chippenham to Bath. By taking this route, he was able to plan a quite remarkably level line. For the first 50 miles, it rises by an average of 1 in 1,320 (4 feet per mile); thereafter to Bristol it is nowhere steeper than 1 in 500, except for two short stretches of 1 in 100, at Wootton Bassett and in the Box Tunnel. His line was later termed 'Brunel's billiard table' for this quality, but some commentators criticised him at the time for taking it through so much empty country.

For nine weeks, Brunel laboured away for up to 20 hours a day, searching for this ideal route, mostly living on horseback, retreating to country inns when the light had faded and working on into the night, snatching a few hours' sleep, then starting again at dawn. William Townshend seems to have faded from the picture within a few weeks: Brunel had become impatient with his comparatively slack working hours. Instead he called on the services of various local surveyors to help him take levels and annotate the Ordnance Survey maps.

By June 1833 he had found his route and delivered the first plans, and on 30 July he presented his proposals to the company's first public meeting, with an initial estimate of £2½ million for the whole line. On 15 August Brunel and seven of the company's directors set out for the capital, where a London Committee was being set up to promote the railway. On 27 August the London and Bristol committees met together for the first time. The newly appointed secretary to the London Committee, Charles Saunders (later the company secretary), was to be perhaps Brunel's most staunch supporter. That same evening, Brunel wrote the initials 'GWR' in his diary for the first time and, shortly after, 'Great Western Railway' became the official title.

With a whole railway to design Brunel needed a permanent base, and he swiftly leased 53 Parliament Street and began to assemble his office staff. He also commissioned a travelling coach or 'britska', large enough to house a bed, a drawing board and instruments, plans, and a large cigar case. For the next nine months, he lived much of the time on the road, negotiating with landowners and directing his growing staff. The pressure of work was intense: he told his senior assistant Hammond, 'between ourselves it is harder work than I like. I am rarely much under twenty hours a day at it'. A diary entry for 14 September 1833 gives some idea what it was like:

Up at 5 a.m. Joined Place & Williams ranged onto the Island east of Caversham. Breakfasted and mounted. Call on Mr Hawks, Surveyor; appointed to be with him at 8 p.m. Rode to meet Hughes; found him in barley stubble west of cottage. Directed him how to proceed and to meet me this evening at the Bear. Rode then to Purley Hall. Met Mr Wilder just going in; spoke to him; found him very civil; gave him a prospectus. Rode on to Basildon Farm; left Mr Hopkins' note and my card on Mr Stone. Rode on to Streatley; tried in every way to find a line round instead of crossing the river at Goring; found it impossible. On looking at the country from the high hill south of Streatley however, it was evident that much cutting might be saved by passing SW of Streatley Farm and winding a little more east of Halfpenny Lane.

Returned to Reading, went in search of Mr Stone; found he was gone. Called on Mr Symonds. Hughes came at 7½. Agreed with him that he was to have £2. 2 a day and pay his own expenses instead of £35 and charges. Pointed out to him the line he was to follow. Took him with me to Mr Hawks to look at his large plan, – Mr H. to furnish him with a copy by tomorrow evening and is to make the survey of the line from Sonning to Streatley inclusive with Book of reference &c. &c. Came to town by mail.

In this way, by January 1834 Brunel and his staff had completed the basic plans, sections and drawings for the whole line, and these were deposited with the Parliamentary Bills office. The GWR were having great difficulty in raising money, so they introduced a bill for the construction of the line from Bristol to Bath, and from London to Reading, promising that the section in the middle would be built later. They met with a storm of opposition: from stagecoach and canal companies, from landowners, from the town of Windsor because they were being bypassed, from the town of Maidenhead because they feared the loss of their bridge tolls from river traffic, and many others. The bill passed its second reading in the Commons on 10 March, then laboured slowly through its committee stage: the engineering evidence lasted for 42 days, of which 11 were devoted entirely to Brunel's cross-examination. However, in August, the bill was thrown out by the House of Lords and the company had to start again. They set about selling more shares, and in the spring of 1835 they introduced a second parliamentary bill to build the whole line to Bristol. This second round lasted another five months, and Brunel faced a second storm of critical questioning. At length the company won through, and the GWR's Act of Parliament received royal assent on 31 August 1835: it had cost them £88,710 in legal and parliamentary fees.

Britain was in a ferment of railway promotion, and the bankers and businessmen who had founded the GWR were already backing proposals for related lines. Brunel, thanks to his superb performance in designing the London to Bristol line, was well placed to be appointed as engineer to these new companies, too. On 31 December 1835, he tallied up his triumphs in his diary, which he had neglected for over a year:

When I last wrote in this book I was just emerging from

obscurity . . . the railway is now in progress. I am their
Engineer to the finest work in England – a handsome salary –
£2,000 a year – on excellent terms with my Directors and all
going smoothly, but what a fight we have had . . .

CLIFTON BRIDGE – my first child – my darling, is
actually going on – commenced work last Monday –
Glorious!

SUNDERLAND DOCKS, too, is going well.

BRISTOL DOCKS. All Bristol is alive and turned bold and
speculative with this railway – we are to widen the entrances
and Lord knows what.

MERTHYR & CARDIFF RAILWAY. This I owe to the
GWR. I care not about it.

CHELTENHAM RAILWAY. Of course I owe this to the
Great Western . . . Do not feel much interested in this. None
of the parties are my friends. I hold it only because they
cannot do without me. It's an awkward line and the
estimate's too low. However, it's all in the way of business
and it's a proud thing to monopolise all the West as I do.

BRISTOL & EXETER RAILWAY. This survey was done in
the grand style – it's a good line too – and I feel an interest as
connected to Bristol to which I really owe much . . . Gravatt
served me well in his B&E survey.

NEWBURY BRANCH. A little go, almost beneath my
notice. It will do as a branch.

SUSPENSION BRIDGE ACROSS THE THAMES [Hunger-
ford footbridge] I have condescended to be engineer of this
but I shan't give myself much trouble about it. If done it will
add to my stock of irons.

I forgot also the Bristol and Gloster Railway.

The defeat of the first bill had at least one very important
consequence. Brunel was given more time to think about the

design of his line and began privately to question the assumption that the rails had to be spaced 4' 8½" apart. He didn't share these thoughts with many others, but he did persuade the chairman of the bills committee to leave out the clause prescribing the gauge from the GWR's Act. In October 1835 he presented his ideas for a broad gauge, with rails seven feet apart, to his directors for the first time: it was a remarkable exercise in thinking from first principles. The 4' 8½" gauge had been adopted by George Stephenson simply because many of the colliery tramways in the north-east were built to that gauge, including the tramway at Killingworth where he built his first locomotive. Brunel automatically questioned such assumptions. He was designing his line to be as straight and level as possible, to achieve fast, smooth running. He reasoned that larger locomotives would be more powerful, that larger wheels run more smoothly than small, and that larger rolling stock could have a lower centre of gravity, making it more stable at high speeds.

All of this, in his view, pointed towards a broader gauge. Brunel's radicalism did not stop there. He invented his own kind of wrought-iron rail, U-shaped in section for lightness and strength, and he started from first principles with his track design as well. The London & Birmingham Railway's rails, like the Liverpool & Manchester's, were set in cast-iron chairs fixed to stone blocks. Brunel proposed that his rails would run on longitudinal timbers, fixed to 'sleepers' running crosswise every 15 feet 6 inches. The timbers would be 'kyanised': treated with a preservative recently invented by a Mr Kyan. The whole framework would be held down on a bed of ballast over hard-rammed sand, with timber piles from 8 to 18 feet long driven into the ground.

Brunel knew every mile of the route, and he controlled the whole design process himself: the assistant engineers were there

to interpret his will. He set out the route; his staff produced
plans, which he checked. Brunel designed most of the buildings
and almost every bridge of any size: the assistants checked and
developed his designs on site. He produced his own estimates for
all of the work, and controlled the letting of contracts. He was
also involved in negotiations with landowners, purchase of
property, and even selling shares.

The line from London to Bristol was divided into sections,
coded by letter: L for London, R for Reading, S for Swindon, C
for Chippenham and B for Bristol. These were subdivided into
contracts, the contracts were let, and work began with the
Wharncliffe Viaduct, over the River Brent at Hanwell, near
Ealing (contract 1L) early in 1836. By the spring of 1837 work
was in progress on much of the line as far as Maidenhead Bridge
(contract 6L). A contract would be let; the route pegged out;
the property would be taken in and fenced; an army of navvies
would arrive on site and commence the task of creating the line,
whether this meant raising an embankment or digging a cutting.
Foundations for viaducts, bridges and culverts would be laid,
supplies of brick and stone got in, and the huge structures
started to go up. It is sobering, when travelling by train now, to
reflect that the huge embankments and cuttings were all dug by
hand, by thousands of navvies. As sheer feats of manual labour,
railways were on an even bigger scale than canals: hardly
anything comparable had been attempted since the time of the
ancient civilisations.

The problems seemed never-ending and at times even Brunel
felt the strain, though he would only admit as much to a few
friends. On 3 December 1837 he wrote to the GWR's secretary,
Charles Saunders:

In my endeavour to introduce a few – really, but a few –
improvements in the principal part of the part, I have

involved myself in a mass of novelties.

I can compare it to nothing but the sudden adoption of a language, familiar enough to the speaker, and, in itself, simple enough, but unfortunately, understood by nobody about him; every word has to be translated. And so it is with my work – one alteration has involved another, and no one part can be copied from what others have done.

I have thus cut myself off from the help usually received from assistants. No one can fill up the details. I am obliged to do all myself, and the quantity of writing, in instructions alone, takes four or five hours a day, and invention is something like a spring of water – limited. I fear I sometimes pump myself dry and remain for an hour or so utterly stupid.

I have spun this long yarn, partly as a recreation after working all the night, principally to have the pleasure of telling a real friend that I am sensible of his kindness, although he hardly allows me to see it . . .

If ever I go mad, I shall have the ghost of the opening of the railway walking before me, or rather standing in front of me, holding out its hand, and when it steps forward, a little swarm of devils in the shape of leavy pickle-tanks, uncut timber, half-finished station houses, sinking embankments, broken screws, absent guard plates, unfinished drawings and sketches, will, quietly and quite as a matter of course and as if I ought to have expected it, lift up my ghost and put him a little further off than before.

These stresses and strains were partly caused by the GWR's having announced in August 1837 that their line would open from London to Maidenhead by the end of the year. This proved to be wildly optimistic: at Christmas, there was still not a single mile of track laid. The London end of the line had, indeed, proved very problematic. The GWR had considered sites at

Paddington and then at Vauxhall for their terminus, but what their Act of Parliament of 1835 provided for was a joint terminus at Euston with the London & Birmingham Railway. At the outset both companies thought that this would be a sensible and workable economy, but in the event they fell out about lease terms, and about the GWR's decision to adopt the broad gauge. The GWR reverted to a site at Paddington, but had to get a second Act of Parliament for this change to their route. Brunel had envisaged a grand terminus there, but the company couldn't afford it, so instead he fitted a temporary station, mostly built of timber, within and around one of his new viaducts, the Bishops Road Bridge.

The spring of 1838 saw a frantic rush to finish the London end and on 31 May the first train, carrying the directors and their guests and with Brunel on the locomotive footplate, ran from Paddington to Maidenhead and back. A few days later, the new railway opened to the public for the first time. However, the feeling of triumph was very short-lived, for Brunel and the GWR had yet to face some of their most difficult trials.

Brunel expected that, as the GWR's engineer, he would control every department of the railway, including the locomotives and rolling stock. His father, after all, had excelled in civil, structural and mechanical engineering, and he expected to do the same. However, at this point his apparent omniscience ran out. He wrote specifications for the GWR's first locomotives with some very striking peculiarities. For example, he ordered that six-wheeled locomotives should not exceed 10½ tons in weight, while four-wheeled locomotives should not exceed 8 tons. This seemed directly to contradict his own remarks about the broad gauge being designed to allow for larger and more powerful engines for heavier engines were already being used in the north of England. As another example, Brunel specified that 30 miles an hour should be the standard speed, at which the maximum piston speed should be 280 feet per minute; yet in the north of England, piston speeds of 500 feet per minute were already being attained. The locomotive manufacturers, obliged to design and build engines to these specifications, produced a motley and underpowered set of machines, some of which could do little more than pull themselves along, and all of which were unreliable.

It is difficult to understand how Brunel arrived at this position: it wasn't for lack of knowledge, as one of his private notebooks of 'Facts' preserved in the National Archive is entirely given over to data concerning locomotives. No one has yet carried out the research needed to reconstruct what he was trying to do. At the time, though, when the railway opened, the results were disastrous. When the GWR's line first opened, they were heavily reliant on two great assets. One was the 'North Star', a locomotive originally built in Newcastle-upon-Tyne by Robert Stephenson & Company for the New Orleans Railway, and converted to the broad gauge after this American company had gone bankrupt. The other was Daniel Gooch, a northern engineer appointed by the GWR to be their locomotive superintendent in 1837, at the age of 21. Gooch, a brilliant mechanical engineer, had to coax Brunel's freak locomotives into running. He was placed in a very uncomfortable position, as the directors initially blamed him for their poor performance. At length, Gooch was obliged to write a report making the nature of the difficulties clear, which caused tension between him and Brunel. Gradually, the problems with the locomotives eased: the GWR took delivery of a fine series of locomotives from Robert Stephenson & Company: the 'Morning Star', 'Rising Star', 'Dog Star' and so on. Later on, Gooch developed his own superb designs, the so-called 'seven foot singles' and 'eight foot singles', named from the diameter of their big driving wheels: they were fast, reliable, and gave many years of good service.

So from May 1838 the GWR was running services and starting to earn some income, but they weren't the fast, smooth-running train services that Brunel had promised. In addition to the trouble with the locomotives, there were problems with his track design, and problems with the carriages. The only consolation for the directors was that the first train services run on the London & Birmingham Railway were every bit as uncomfortable. There had been an assumption, shared by Brunel and the Stephensons, that the track needed to be anchored down and held rigid, whether by Brunel's timber piles or by the Stephensons' stone blocks. They were mistaken, and soon there was a general realisation that the track needed to have some 'give' in it to absorb some of the impact and shocks generated by the locomotive. So the timber piles had to come out again and the track had to be re-ballasted and relaid, and meanwhile Gooch was struggling with the failing locomotives, and the company was trying to get its services running with some degree of reliability, and Brunel and his staff were working to extend the line westwards, and all the time the costs were soaring, far above his initial estimates.

Criticisms of Brunel mounted through 1838, and the most vehement critics tended to come from the GWR's northern shareholders, the so-called 'Liverpool Party'. There was a significant group of Liverpudlian investors behind many of the early railway companies: indeed, at the outset, both the London & Birmingham Railway and the Grand Junction Railway (which linked it to the Liverpool & Manchester) were more or less controlled from that northern city. These rich investors had experienced the building and running of the first railways in the north of England: they trusted the down-to-earth approach of George Stephenson and his 4' 8½" gauge, and increasingly, they distrusted Brunel. The GWR's management was besieged by a large and powerful body of shareholders. The crisis came towards the end of the year, when the company invited outside experts in to advise, and they were highly criticial of the broad gauge: in November and December, Brunel came close to resigning. Speed trials using the reliable 'North Star' at the beginning of 1839 helped to turn the argument, and on 7 January Saunders and the directors won the crucial vote against the Liverpool opposition by 7,790 votes to 6,145. Brunel and the broad gauge were saved.

Meanwhile, the line had been growing westwards from Maidenhead. From Berkshire into Wiltshire it rises gently, with relatively few major engineering works, and the GWR was able to open the line by stages to Twyford in May 1839, to Reading in March 1840, to Faringdon Road in July, and to Wootton Bassett in December. By this time Brunel and Daniel Gooch had picked the small market town of Swindon, nearby, as the site for the GWR's 'principal engine establishment', it being close to the summit of the line. The major work to build this was delayed until after the opening, but from 1841 a great series of workshops began to rise to Brunel's and Gooch's designs, ranged around three sides of a 540-foot-square courtyard: this was the start of Swindon's history as a great railway and manufacturing town. At the time there was nowhere for a workforce to live, so in 1842 Brunel also produced drawings for 'New Swindon', a model village of Tudor-style cottages on a rectangular street plan: the original 'railway village' still stands today.

Swindon's station was endowed with 'refreshment rooms', the GWR's idea being that passengers would want something to eat and this was a convenient place to provide it. By this time the company was very short of funds, so they struck a deal with a firm of building contractors, J. & C. Rigby, who undertook to build the station as well as the railway village in return for the revenue they would earn, including that from this early catering concession. All the trains stopped at Swindon, and there was only one place to eat. Thus a grand British tradition of bad railway food was born, and the complaints poured in, including this riposte from Brunel himself:

Dear Sir,

I assure you Mr Player was wrong in supposing that I thought you purchased inferior coffee. I thought I said to him I was surprised you should buy such bad roasted corn. I did not believe you had such a thing as coffee in the place; I am certain I never tasted any. I have long ceased to make complaints at Swindon. I avoid taking anything there when I can help it.

Yours faithfully, I. K. Brunel.

The western end of the line, from Bristol to Bath, had made much slower progress: it ran through more difficult terrain with a series of short tunnels alongside the Avon, and the work was dogged by foul weather and by the bankruptcy of William Ranger, one of the main contractors. Nevertheless, the Bristol Committee, which was overseeing this end of the line, was much more generous in its allocations for architecture than the London Committee, so Brunel was able to endow his tunnels with a splendid series of castellated portals built from the local stone, and at Bristol Temple Meads he was able to carry out his grand Tudor Gothic design for the station, in contrast to the temporary affair at Paddington.

The great timber roof, 72 feet across, was adorned with 'hammerbeams', but in reality these were only for show. It was a daringly novel design in which the roof was carried by pairs of cantilevered beams balanced over the columns (imagine a pair of tower cranes, their booms angled upwards, facing each other). The point of this seems to have been that Brunel wanted a clear span, without columns cluttering up his train-shed, but it would have been very difficult and prohibitively expensive to build a conventional timber truss 72 feet wide. However, it seems to have run into difficulties while still under construction. The problem seems to have been that the timber declined to behave with the requisite degree of stiffness: the roof quickly showed signs of stress, and it had all to be tied together with wrought-iron straps and a lot of hidden strengthening.

The line opened from Bristol to Bath in August 1840. This left the most difficult section of the entire line, from there to Chippenham. For 13 miles scarcely one mile of the line is within 10 feet of the natural surface: it all had to be raised on embankments, or sunk in cuttings, or, worst of all, tunnelled. The Box Tunnel, 1¾ miles long through solid rock, had always been the most controversial element of Brunel's design, and its construction was the most traumatic chapter of the whole story. Trial shafts were sunk in 1836, and eight construction shafts were begun in 1837, but it proved difficult to persuade contractors to tender for the main work. In February 1838, George Burge of Herne Bay agreed to take the major, western part, while two local contractors, Lewis and Brewer, took the eastern half-mile. Marc Brunel's tunnelling shield was of no help through solid rock, and the working conditions were, if anything, worse than those in the Thames Tunnel, albeit in an entirely different way. The rock had to be broken by gunpowder, before it could be attacked by the miners with picks, working day after day in the hot, damp, unventilated, fume-filled darkness. The workings flooded repeatedly. The spoil had to be winched up the great shafts, ranging from 70 to 300 feet deep, by horses turning gins. The miners had to get to work in baskets lowered down the same shafts. This went on for three years: 1,100 men and 100 horses. In the last six months, Brunel urged Burge to increase the workforce to 4,000: a ton of candles and a ton of gunpowder were consumed each week. In March

1841 this appalling epic was brought to a conclusion, at a cost of over a hundred men's lives. At last, the line opened from London to Bristol, with a startling lack of ceremony, on 30 June 1841.

By this time the GWR's empire had expanded greatly, and in fact, their trains could already run a lot further, to Bridgwater in Somerset on the allied Bristol & Exeter line.

Brunel's responsibilities had grown, as the GWR acquired more subsidiary or allied companies, all of which appointed him as their engineer, and almost all of which adopted the broad gauge. As he wrote in his diary in December 1835, 'it's a proud thing to monopolise all the West, as I do', but the work piled up relentlessly.

There was much more to come, for the first railway lines turned out to be very profitable, and in the 1840s there was a tremendous surge of proposals for new lines: the 'Railway Mania'. The GWR emerged as one of the three leading companies: it extended the broad gauge to the far West via the South Devon Railway, the Cornwall Railway and the West Cornwall Railway. It expanded into Wales via the Gloucester and Dean Forest Railway and the South Wales Railway. It spread into the Midlands via a branch to Oxford, and the Oxford, Worcester & Wolverhampton Railway, and the Birmingham & Oxford Junction. There were more: too many to be enumerated here. Brunel was appointed as chief engineer to all of them. He could not maintain the same degree of personal involvement in surveying and designing the lines as he had for the London to Bristol route, not least because he had to spend so much time, in these years, as a witness before parliamentary committees. Nevertheless he continued, to a remarkable degree, to control both the design and construction of these lines through his assistant engineers. By the time Brunel died over 1,200 miles of railway had been built in England and Wales to his design or under his direct supervision.

In 1845 the 'Gauge War' broke out. The GWR faced serious opposition, for the 4' 8½" gauge camp was led by two formidable companies, both formed by mergers in 1845: the Midland Railway and the London & North Western. They bitterly opposed the GWR's bids to carry the broad gauge into the Midlands, and the battle raged, on the stock exchanges and in parliamentary committee rooms, for almost two years. The GWR secured Acts of Parliament for their new lines, but an official commission was set up to investigate the whole matter. Brunel persuaded them to carry out speed trials, to compare the speed and quality of Gooch's broad-gauge locomotives to a standard-gauge rival, and the GWR's engine won this hands down; but speed alone was not enough. Early in 1846 the commission reported, and for Brunel and the GWR the news was bad. It was acknowledged that broad-gauge trains were faster, but these express services were seen as primarily being for the first class passengers. What clinched matters was that by 1846, 274 miles of broad-gauge line was in operation, as compared to 1,901 miles of standard gauge. For general service, the 4' 8½" gauge would do perfectly well and was to be regarded as the industry standard for new lines. The GWR managed to negotiate a let-out clause: new railways could still be laid to something other than 4' 8½", if a case could be made, but even so they were on the defensive.

At the outset, Brunel had tried to argue that having two railway gauges in one country would work, as the broad gauge would serve a self-contained area. By 1846 the two systems had met and the inconvenience caused was all too obvious. He had probably assumed that his system would be so plainly superior that eventually everyone else would convert to it. In reality, this was never going to happen, and after 1846, for the GWR to expand, it had to buy standard-gauge lines and then lay mixed-gauge tracks so that it could run both kinds of train. The writing was on the wall for Brunel's heroic vision: the bitter truth was that George Stephenson had got there first.

By this time Brunel was pursuing another dream of technical innovation: the South Devon Atmospheric Railway. The broad gauge has never lacked its champions and, indeed, there were always good technical arguments in its favour. Unfortunately the same was not true of the atmospheric railway, and this has always been regarded as the worst fiasco of his entire career. The idea grew out of the difficult terrain involved: Brunel had surveyed a fairly level line for the South Devon company, running behind Torquay, but they couldn't afford the heavy earthworks involved. So instead he planned a line which wound around the coast, which would be cheaper to build, but slower to run. The company obtained their Act of Parliament in July 1844. That September, Brunel, Gooch and others witnessed a demonstration of atmospheric traction on the Kingston to Dalkey Railway, a very short (1½ mile) line near Dublin: a 'piston carriage' hauled a train of two coaches up a 1 in 120 slope, smoothly and silently, at 28 miles per hour. Brunel was impressed, thinking that he had found the solution to the South Devon company's problems, and when work on the line began in 1845 it was built to run on this new system.

The system had been patented by two London engineers, William Clegg and Jacob Samuda, in 1838. A trial stretch of line was laid on Wormwood Scrubs, and was successful enough to lead to its being adopted by the Kingston to Dalkey line, and for the London to Croydon Railway, so Brunel was not alone in being impressed. Clegg & Samuda's system ran off a pipe, about 9 inches in diameter, running along the track, with a slot running along it, closed by a hinged metal cover, with a leather flap to act as a valve or seal. The piston filled the pipe, and was attached by a stout arm to the piston carriage. A stationary steam engine would pump the air out of the pipe ahead of the piston, creating a vacuum. The piston – and the carriage – would be pulled forward by the vacuum. The crucial point was that as soon as the piston had passed, the flap should fall back into place to maintain an airtight seal. If the seal leaked the vacuum would fail, and the whole thing would grind to a halt.

On an optimistic reading, the system seemed to have a lot going for it. It was clean and silent. For traction it didn't depend on the weight of a locomotive gripping the rails, as there was no locomotive, so everything could be more lightly constructed and it could cope with steeper gradients, potentially saving a lot of money on the cost of building the line: but there was an even bigger point than this. Brunel had realised that a great deal of the energy used in pulling a railway train was consumed in moving the weight of the locomotive itself. His colleague Daniel Gooch made detailed experiments on locomotive efficiency during the gauge war controversy, and came to the astonishing conclusion that at 40 miles an hour one third of the power generated by the locomotive was used to move its own weight, and at 60 miles an hour that proportion rose to a half. Brunel thought that a system in which the power came from a stationary engine and was transmitted as a vacuum down a simple tube, with less energy lost in friction, could be dramatically more efficient.

Even at the outset, though, Brunel must have known that the atmospheric system had formidable shortcomings. The system depended on the efficiency of the pumping engines: if one failed, the whole system closed down. The vacuum was being created by an engine house which might be several miles away: how would the power supply be coordinated with train movements? The pipe had to be flat and continuous, so how could one manage the inclusion of points, or junctions, or crossings? Worst of all, and the absolute Achilles heel of the whole system, was the need to maintain a perfect seal. Gooch and the Stephensons remained sceptical throughout, but Brunel was convinced that the problems could be overcome, and that a new form of light transport would be the result. This was the future.

The first section of the South Devon line, from Exeter to Teignmouth, opened in 1846. For the first year it was worked by conventional locomotives, but Brunel was making preparations to install Clegg & Samuda's system: he designed a series of engine houses in a charming Italianate style for the stationary steam engines. Atmospheric propulsion began in August 1847, and in February 1848 it was extended to Newton Abbot: the experiment lasted for just over a year. Test services with light loads had reached speeds of up to 35 miles an hour, but the everyday reality turned out to be sadly different. Getting the engines to produce a vacuum at the right moments was rendered easier by the installation of a telegraph system in February 1848. Maintaining the vacuum consistently, however, seemed to be impossible. The seal or valve was made of leather, caulked with grease. In the summer it dried out, which was bad enough: in the winter it froze solid, which was worse (and there is a hardy Devon myth, which may have a kernel of truth, that the leather was eaten by rats). A small army of men had to be employed simply to keep the valve greased. Atmospheric propulsion was estimated to be costing the company 37 pence per mile, as opposed to 16 pence for locomotive propulsion. There would doubtless have been many other problems, for example relating to inadequate horsepower, maximum train weights and the difficulty of introducing points, but the system didn't last long enough for these to be fully manifested.

The South Devon directors called on Brunel at Duke Street to hear his explanations on 1 August 1848, and on 19 August he accepted defeat, acknowledging that the system should not be extended any further. The experiment was over very quickly, and the railway was converted to locomotive traction. At least

Brunel knew when to call a halt, though this was probably of
little consolation to the South Devon shareholders, who
between them had lost over £400,000. It is easy to understand
his desire to make this system work but still, as Gooch
remarked:

> I could not understand how Mr Brunel could be so misled. He
> had so much faith in his being able to improve it that he shut
> his eyes to the consequences of failure.

It was the heaviest blow to his reputation that Brunel ever
endured, but his career was too solidly founded to be shaken by
it. By 1850 the Railway Mania had subsided, though a number of
the lines promoted back in the 1840s were still under
construction, beneath the watchful and controlling eye of Duke
Street. Still, the pace of work at home had fallen off markedly,
and like other British engineers and contractors, Brunel was
now looking overseas for work.

In the 1850s there was, doubtless, more demand for
engineers' services from overseas, but working abroad was an
uncertain business. Brunel sent an assistant engineer to produce
a survey for the Piedmont Railway, but this fizzled out (1843–4).
His office designed the Florence to Pistoia Railway, which was
built c. 1844–8, but by the time it was finished the Duchy of
Tuscany was embroiled in revolution, and Brunel was never paid
in full. He had a role, at more of an arm's length, in the planning
of the East Bengal Railway (1855–9) and the Melbourne to
Williamstown Railway (1858–9).

In the end, railway building all came down to money, and
when the Railway Mania of 1846 subsided, and the stockmarket
boom turned to bust, much of Brunel's work – and his peers' –
dried up, which is why they had to turn their attention overseas.
Brunel has often been described as extravagant, careless with his

shareholders' money but is this really fair? The GWR's main line went a long way over budget, costing over £6 million against his initial estimate of £2½ million, but the same was true of many of the first railways, and reflected the degree to which these huge projects were a leap in the dark. Real courage was required, and in the end it was usually rewarded. The GWR paid its first dividend, of 3%, in 1841, and over the next decade, during which it was building and expanding continuously, it nevertheless returned an annual dividend of between 3 and 8%. In 1841 the GWR, which had cost £6,678,000 to build, had a stockmarket value of £8,390,000: the biggest company, the London & Birmingham, had cost £6,091,000 to build, and was worth £13,378,000, but this was an exceptionally good performance. Brunel's critics produced endless claims about the extra cost of the broad-gauge lines, the GWR cost £56,300 per mile, higher but not spectacularly higher than the London & Birmingham, at £53,100, or the Liverpool & Manchester, at £51,000. Brunel was as well aware of the value of money as anyone: and no one who has looked at his correspondence with the GWR's contractors would say for one moment that he erred in their favour. If the GWR was expensive, this was because of Brunel's insistence on the highest standards of materials and execution: this was, after all, to be the 'finest work in England'.

5

Brunel's Bridges

Britain has only a few large rivers and thus, until the Industrial Revolution, presented relatively few opportunities (or demands) for bridges of any great ambition. Most of them were based on simple arched designs and it is broadly true to say that until the late 18th century bridge building in Britain, at its best, remained a long way short of the achievements of the ancient Romans.

The situation started to change in the late 18th century thanks to two main factors. The first was the development of the new turnpike roads and canals which spread across the landscape in the late 18th and early 19th centuries: the engineering profession found themselves required to build great numbers of new bridges. In the early 1800s a number of large and magnificent masonry bridges went up, like John Rennie's Waterloo Bridge in London (1811–17), or Thomas Harrison's Grosvenor Bridge at Chester (1827–33).

The second factor was the development of iron as a bridging material. In 1781 Abraham Darby III opened the world's first iron bridge at Ironbridge, whose cast-iron sections make up a clear span of 100 feet. As an achievement of design and iron founding it was so ambitious and so far ahead of its time that it was some years before anyone attempted anything comparable. Nevertheless, a barrier had been broken, and in 1796 Thomas Wilson raised the stakes further by completing his astonishing bridge over the Wear at Sunderland, a single cast-iron arch spanning 236 feet. Other fine cast-iron bridges followed on quickly. Canal aqueducts presented a particular opportunity in this respect: the most spectacular example is Jessop's and Telford's Pontcysyllte Aqueduct in Denbighshire of 1794–1805, a thousand feet long, with its cast-iron trough up to 121 feet above the river. At Pontcysyllte, and in his Menai suspension bridge of 1819–26, Telford demonstrated that he was the leader of the field, the foremost road and bridge builder of his age, but several other engineers were working at the frontiers of knowledge too. So when Brunel began designing his railway in 1835 he was operating in a competitive, fast-moving situation, with a lot of new ideas about bridge design and the structural uses of iron in the air.

Brunel's role as engineer to the Great Western Railway and

its allied companies involved designing and building hundreds of bridges: no one knows how many, and Brunel himself probably couldn't have said. The construction of railways – even more than canals – raised new problems and issues. First there was the overriding need to keep the line as straight and as level as possible, even if this meant raising it on embankments or sinking it in cuttings for mile after mile. Then there was the inescapable fact that they were operating in a mature, occupied landscape, that was already full of roads, canals, navigable rivers, and property interests of all kinds: they all had to be respected and accommodated. When approaching a sizeable town or city, the engineer was often obliged to decide whether he was going to take his line below the streets in cuttings, or over them on viaducts. All of this helps explain why railway building involved unprecedented amounts of bridge building, and why railways were so frighteningly expensive.

And yet it all happened so quickly. It is doubtful whether any previous society in history could have simultaneously marshalled the financial liquidity, the armies of labour, and the organisational and engineering skills to do anything on this scale in such a short space of time, and certainly not without relying on slave labour (this is apart from the fact that no previous society could have developed the technology anyway). For Victorian Britain built not one railway line, but dozens – and then went on to finance and organise railway building in every continent in the world.

Brunel began the GWR's main line with a bridge: work began on the 300-yard-long Wharncliffe Viaduct over the shallow valley of the River Brent at Hanwell in West London, in February 1836. Brunel had worked out the geometry of the eight beautiful elliptical brick arches, each 72 feet wide, in one of his notebooks, but he seems to have had a good deal of help from his father, Marc, whose diaries for the spring of 1834 included numerous entries for 'working on Isambard's Brent Viaduct'.

Most of the many bridges on the GWR's London to Bristol line were of brick or stone, and most were relatively straightforward. Many of Brunel's original over-line bridges still remain in service, instantly recognisable by their elegant elliptical arches. At Maidenhead, however, a major problem presented itself, as Brunel had to get his line across the 100-yard-wide Thames while providing enough clearance for the sailing barges. He was already having to raise the line on huge embankments, and wanted to avoid putting a 'hump' in it which would have interrupted the gentle 1 in 1,320 gradient. There was a little island in the midstream, and Brunel's solution was to design the two widest brick arches that had ever been built, each spanning 128 feet, landing on a central pier on the island. The tight vertical constraints meant that the arches had to be kept very shallow, rising by just 28 feet. Arches are complex structures, and still not fully understood: when arch design is pushed this far, the weight distribution within the structure becomes critical.

By the summer of 1838 the bridge was nearing completion. One of the many critical factors in building a brick or stone arch is the length of time needed for the mortar to set: if it is still soft when the timber centring is lowered, the structure may settle. The contractor William Chadwick without Brunel's permission had the timber centring of one of the arches eased somewhat too soon, and the brickwork sank slightly: a gap of about half an inch appeared between the lowest three courses around the centre of the arch. The centring was still in place, and Brunel ordered the contractor to jack it back up and make good the defective area at his own expense. However, the affair became known about: this was at the time when Brunel was at his most vulnerable to the critics, and it was used by the Liverpool Party as a stick with which to beat him. The bridge was repaired to Brunel's design and he has been absolutely vindicated: the Maidenhead Bridge has been carrying railway traffic every day since 1839.

Maidenhead Bridge still has the widest and flattest brick arches in Britain (if not the world). None of Brunel's other masonry bridges were quite so ambitious, but he did design several other very large arches in the early stages of his railway work. There are big bridges with 62-foot arches over the Thames at Gathampton and Moulsford. There is an 86-foot span at Bathford, and an 88-foot span at Bath. More daringly, he built a 120-foot stone arch with a rise of a mere 20 feet to carry the line over the 'New Cut' of the Avon in Bristol: its crown sank 'much more than was expected', but even so, it stood safely for 80 years and proved extremely difficult to demolish when the time came to replace it in the 1920s. Just one of his many masonry bridges went seriously wrong. This was a very low-pitched arch, 100 feet wide and with a rise of only 12 feet, carrying the Bristol & Exeter line over the river Parrett near Bridgwater in Somerset, built in 1838–41. The thrust of the arch started gradually pushing the abutments outwards in the soft ground, and Brunel could not risk removing the timber centring. The centring, however, was blocking navigation on the river, and Brunel was obliged to remove the arch and replace it with a timber structure, which then did duty until 1904. This was one of the only two failures in all his hundreds of bridges, neither of which caused a collapse, let alone a fatality, and both of which he coped with successfully.

Brunel designed all the bridges on the London to Bristol line himself: they were all designed individually, except for the simpler over-line arches, which seem to be to a standard pattern. Later on, as his responsibilities grew, he developed more of these standard designs, which his staff could then adapt to specific locations. He had a quite outstanding grasp of the way structures behave, but this was not just instinctive: every one of these designs was worked out mathematically. Brunel was using scientific theory – what is now termed 'elementary statics' – which had originated in the 17th century, but the theory was continuing to develop, and he himself contributed to this. His notebooks contain page after page of detailed calculations for arches, including those for Maidenhead and the Wharncliffe Viaduct. The sheer amount of work just in his bridge designs is mind-boggling.

One of Brunel's great aims was to make the structures as light as possible: partly to economise on materials, and also to achieve the most efficient distribution of the stresses. One of his many insights was that all materials without exception, even granite, have some degree of flexibility. The key to bridge design was to understand how the weight would be distributed: how the stresses would be transferred through the structure. In 1854 he wrote to an assistant, William Bell to explain:

> You cannot take too much pains in making everything in equilibrio; that is to say, that all forces should pass exactly through the points of greater resistance, or through the centres of any surfaces of resistance. Thus, in anything resembling a column or strut, whether of iron, wood, or masonry, take care that the surface of the base should be proportioned that the strain should pass through the centre of it. Consider all structures, and all bodies, and all materials of foundations to be made of very elastic india-rubber, and proportion them so that they will stand and keep their shape: you will by these means diminish greatly the required thickness: *then add 50 per cent.*

An oil painting by F. Moore illustrating the 'Cornishman', the last broad-gauge express to run from London to Penzance, 20 May 1892.

J.C. Bourne's magnificent view of the Maidenhead Bridge. Brunel was obliged to leave a clearance of 28 feet above the Thames for the masts of sailing barges, and responded by designing the two widest and flattest brick arches that have ever been built. The bridge was doubled in width on the far (north) side in the 1870s, but Brunel's design was carefully replicated. His original arches are still in service, carrying railway trains every day.

EARLY LOCOMOT
GREAT WESTERN RAIL

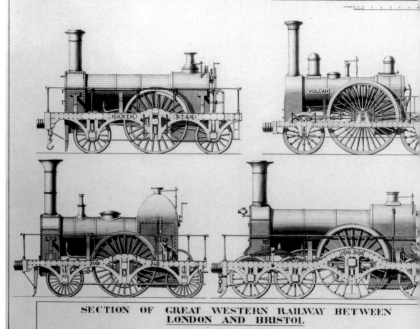

SECTION OF GREAT WESTERN RAILWAY BETWEEN
LONDON AND BRISTOL

Horizontal Scale one quarter inch to a mile

Vertical Scale one hundred and sixty feet to an in

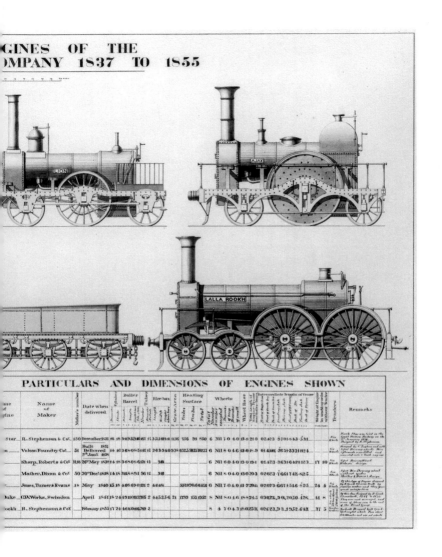

The GWR's major classes of locomotives from its early years. Stephenson's 'North Star' was followed by several sisters, all named after stars. The next three, the 'Vulcan', 'Lion' and 'Ajax' represent the engines made to Brunel's unorthodox specifications in 1837–8, which mostly gave poor, unreliable service. The three bigger engines on the bottom row were all designed by Daniel Gooch. At first they were made by several manufacturers until the GWR works at Swindon grew big enough to meet all of the company's demand. The 'Firefly' was particularly successful with 63 engines built.

The Ivybridge Viaduct on the South Devon Atmospheric Railway: a watercolour by J.C. Bourne, though not painted for his *History of the Great Western Railway*. When it was first built, to support the light loads of the atmospheric railway, the deck was carried on the raking beams. When Brunel had to convert it for full-time locomotive traffic he added the upper tier of timber work, which looks like a form of balustrade, to provide additional strength.

Treviddo Viaduct: one of the 43 timber viaducts that Brunel designed and built for the Cornwall and West Cornwall Railways in 1850–9. The fans of raking beams and the way they merge into the trussed bridge deck represent the ultimate development of the ideas that he first developed for the bridge at Sonning. This viaduct was replaced in masonry in 1898.

This photograph shows the Saltash Bridge in the summer of 1858, shortly after the second truss had been floated into position.

The SS *Great Britain* had been built in a dry dock on the south side of the Floating Harbour, so her launch essentially consisted of the dock sluices being opened at the moment that the Prince Consort broke the customary bottle over her bows. Six hundred guests had just been entertained to a banquet on board.

The SS *Great Western* passing Portishead, immediately after leaving the Avon on her maiden voyage to New York, 8 April 1838: an oil painting by J. Walters.

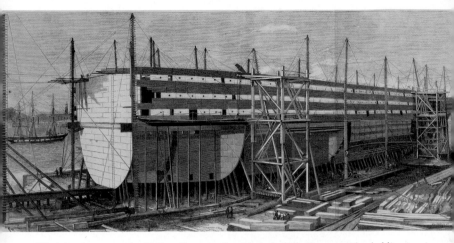

Work in progress on the SS *Great Eastern* c.1855. Note the lack of cranes. The cladding is going on from the top down, and the transverse bulkheads are still visible in the lower part of the hull.

Brunel on board the SS *Great Eastern* on 2 September 1859. This is the last photograph ever taken of him: his illness has clearly taken a heavy toll.

From about 1839, Brunel began to develop a language of design for timber bridges as well. Before long he had developed an absolute mastery of the material, and he has been described as arguably the greatest timber engineer that Britain has ever seen. The tragedy is that not a single timber bridge by him survives: the material just doesn't last that long, or at any rate, not safely, and not in this kind of structure. However, the whole point of the timber bridges was that they were cheap to build, though expensive to maintain: they were a way of getting cash-strapped companies up and running. Brunel expected them to have a short shelf-life, and to be replaced.

He started with two timber bridges on the London to Bristol main line. One carried a road over the Sonning cutting: the road deck was carried on four tall trestles, via a series of radiating struts: this was the starting point for a whole series of viaduct designs. The Skew Bridge over the Avon in Bath was more of a one-off. At Maidenhead, the design problem was to do with heights and levels. Here, the problem had to do with the angle at which the railway crossed the river.

In the old pre-railway days, the obvious thing for a bridge designer to do was to span the river or road or whatever by the shortest route possible, with the bridge at right angles to the obstacle. When planning a railway, on the other hand, there was an overriding need to keep the line as straight as possible, so railway builders were always having to cross roads, rivers and canals at awkward angles, and the skew bridge was born. Building one in brick involved craftsmanship of a high order, as the courses have to be laid to a slope. Building one in stone was an even more complicated business, as all the stones in the arch had to be cut to size specially in order for the sloping courses to fit together. Britain is full of fine 19th-century masonry skew bridges; most of them would strike the casual passer-by as just another rather grimy-looking railway arch; actually, they represent sophisticated pieces of design and craftsmanship which today's building industry would have difficulty reproducing, and then only at a huge cost. Brunel must have designed dozens of them: we don't know how many.

The Avon Bridge in Bath provides a good illustration of why large skew bridges could be complicated. It has two spans, and measured square to the river (that is, at right angles to it) they are only 35 feet across, but the railway crosses the river at such a sharply skewed angle that measured on the line of the track the spans are actually 87 feet long. Brunel wanted to build the bridge in cast iron, but he was unable to let the contract, and instead chose to use laminated timber, making six sets of timber arches for each span.

Laminated timber, in essence, means two or more layers of wood glued or bolted together. Engineers had long known that the depth of a beam is a critical factor in its load-bearing capacity: a beam 24 feet long and 24 inches deep can bear four times the load of a beam 24 feet long and 12 inches deep. The great problem, of course, was finding trees big enough to yield really large beams. So the solution was to fix two or more beams together, one on top of another. The great problem was that, for this to work, you have to guarantee that the beams are fixed together solidly throughout their length. You can span a wider gap with an arch than with a beam, and other British railway engineers had begun to experiment with laminated timber arches: what Brunel designed at Bath was ambitious without being revolutionary: his arches were made up of five layers or laminations, each 6 inches thick, of Baltic pine, bent into shape and fixed together with iron bolts and straps. The spandrels of the outer arches were filled with decorative iron framing, resembling Gothic tracery. This fine bridge lasted 38 years.

The next big opportunity came when the GWR and its satellite companies ran a railway line from Swindon via

Cheltenham to Gloucester: Brunel designed nine timber bridges on the line, including one with a single span of 67 feet at Bourne and another with a span of 75 feet at St Mary's (both over the Thames & Severn Canal). In both cases, there wasn't much clearance available over the canal, certainly not enough for timber arches as in Bath. So Brunel designed ingenious timber trusses tied together below with wrought-iron straps. This was the start of a long saga of design development, in which he repeatedly displayed remarkable powers of invention.

First there were five viaducts on the South Devon Railway, built in 1843–7. The biggest of these, at Ivybridge, had eleven openings each 61 feet wide with a maximum height of 104 feet. Brunel gave these viaducts a uniform design, carried on tall, slender masonry piers, and because he was only expecting to support the light carriages of the atmospheric railway, he designed a slender bridge deck of laminated timber carried on baulks which fanned out from the top of the piers, a little like the bridge at Sonning. When the railway was converted to locomotive use, Brunel had to strengthen the viaducts to carry heavier loads, and found a cheap way to do so by adding an extra tier of trusses in place of the parapets. Later he designed another six timber viaducts for the Tavistock Branch of the South Devon Railway, opened in 1859.

In the late 1840s, Brunel was supervising the Oxford, Worcester & Wolverhampton Railway, and the Birmingham & Oxford Junction. He endowed both of them with large numbers of timber bridges, including some sizeable viaducts carried on timber trestles: for the actual spans, he was mostly using simple triangular trusses in which the timber principals are tied together with wrought-iron straps and bolts, probably based on his earlier roof designs.

Brunel had been appointed as engineer to the South Wales Railway in 1844: it received its Act of Parliament in 1846 and building continued for the next ten years and more. The line had to cross deep valleys and wide estuaries and the South Wales Railway, too, was strapped for cash. Brunel designed a host of timber bridges for them, including his two longest. The Usk Viaduct at Newport was 1,200 feet long, in 11 timber spans with a 100-foot central span: it was damaged by fire during construction in 1848, by which time Brunel was able to replace it in wrought iron. The Landore Viaduct, over a valley near Swansea, was even more ambitious: 580 yards long with 37 spans, carried on tall timber trestles. There had to be a central span, 100 feet wide, over the river. How was it possible to do this to carry railway loads, in wood, given the difficulty of obtaining sound, straight pieces of timber above 30 feet in length? Brunel solved the problem with geometry, designing a new kind of polygonal truss, which might be described as one arch within another.

Brunel's culminating achievement as a timber engineer was the 43 viaducts he designed for the Cornwall Railway and the West Cornwall Railway between 1850 and 1859. His work in Cornwall is one of the most effective answers to the accusation that he was careless with shareholders' money. It was a poor county, but its beautiful, undulating landscape was challenging for a railway engineer. The timber viaducts were part of a carefully thought-out strategy to build the railways as cheaply as possible, get them running, and upgrade the lines as and when money was available. The West Cornwall Railway, from Truro to Penzance, came first: it had a head start in that it incorporated the Hayle Railway, a standard-gauge line from Redruth to Hayle built for minerals traffic which represented about a third of the route. The company were very short of money, so Brunel completed the line as a single track of standard-gauge line, which could be converted to the mixed gauge later. The total cost, including nine timber viaducts, was £105,000, and it opened in August 1852.

The Cornwall Railway, from Truro to Plymouth, was a much more complicated proposition. Brunel had become their engineer, displacing Captain W. E. Moorsom, in 1845, and his design secured parliamentary approval the same year. Work began in 1847, but stopped again when the money ran out. In 1851 Brunel told the board that if they laid a single line of broad-gauge rails to start with, he could finish it for £800,000, including the Saltash Bridge over the Tamar. The 53 miles of line included 34 timber viaducts with an aggregate length of over five miles, which gives some idea of just how difficult the terrain was. His designs for the viaducts went through several generations, from simple trestles supporting laminated timber beams as at Penponds, to trestles carrying trussed beams as at the 1,134 foot-long Nottar Viaduct, to trestles with timber 'fans' supporting the deck, as at Angarrack. For the deeper valleys, trestles would not do, and Brunel designed a series of spectacular viaducts carried on tall masonry piers: the biggest of these, at Moorswater, was 954 feet long with a maximum height of 147 feet. The highest, at St Pinnock, had a maximum height of 151 feet. All the viaducts were marvels of economical design, but the tall viaducts in particular, with their slender buttressed piers, their framing made from long baulks of kyanised pine, set in cast-iron shoes and tied together with wrought-iron rods, were spectacular as well. While the directors were grateful (and they certainly should have been), the passengers were often terrified: the trains had to slow down to cross the viaducts, and the creaking and flexing of the slender structures must have been audible and alarming. Brunel knew, and warned the company, that they would cost a lot to maintain, but this was all part of the bargain. Gradually they were replaced, but the last of them, at Collegewood, remained in service until 1934.

Some of Brunel's most famous achievements as a bridge builder are in iron, but he got off to a slow start with the material by comparison with his friend and rival Robert Stephenson, who in the 1830s was building large numbers of cast-iron bridges on the London & Birmingham Railway. Brunel experienced serious problems with his first iron bridge at the Uxbridge Road in Hanwell, West London. The railway had to cross a turnpike road (two roads crossing each other, in fact) at a fiercely skewed angle. The angle was too sharp for brick arches to be possible, so Brunel produced an elaborate design with a great frame of iron girders carried on massive brick abutments and two rows of columns. This was the second place where one has to acknowledge that one of his bridge designs failed. One of the iron beams broke during construction in 1837; it was replaced, and several rounds of load testing were carried out; a beam broke again a year after the railway had opened in 1839. Then, in 1847, the bridge deck caught fire, the ironwork was damaged, and it had to be completely rebuilt.

There are a couple of well-known and emphatic quotations in which Brunel expressed his distrust of cast iron and these have led many authors to assume that he hardly ever used the material. In fact, there is reason to believe that he designed over fifty cast-iron bridges. Cast iron is produced by heating pig iron to melting point, then pouring it into a mould formed by pressing timber 'patterns' into casting sand. There were limitations to the size and shape of the mould, and to the maximum size that a casting could be before serious flaws developed in the iron. Cast iron is, in any case, a brittle material, strong in compression but weak in tension (meaning, roughly speaking, that it doesn't like being pulled or bent). This is why Brunel distrusted the material, so when he produced his own beam-designs for bridges on the GWR he tested them with his characteristic thoroughness, and then carried out further rounds of experimental work to try and find the ideal shapes for beams. Most of his cast-iron bridges have long since been replaced, but an interesting early example, a road bridge spanning the canal near Paddington Station, was rediscovered in 2003. Another survivor is the 'Windmill Bridge' in Hanwell, West London: a canal aqueduct with a cast-iron trough dating from 1858. There may be more waiting to be found, and more research is needed for us to understand this aspect of Brunel's career properly.

Other engineers, notably Robert Stephenson and his collaborators, were to make bigger and bigger cast-iron beams, up to spans of about 100 feet, until disaster struck with the Dee Bridge collapse of 1847. Brunel supported his friend in the subsequent inquiry, but must have felt that his own more cautious approach had been vindicated.

In the 1840s it was becoming clear that cast iron could be replaced as a large-scale bridging material, as the techniques for making and using wrought iron were developing quickly. Until the 18th century wrought iron was the blacksmith's material, made by hammering pig iron in a red- or white-hot state into bar form, and working it over and over again so that the material lost some of its carbon content and became more ductile (capable of bending without breaking). This could normally only be done on a small scale – the scale of a blacksmith's forge. In the early 18th century 'trip hammers' were developed to forge wrought iron on a bigger scale, but the crucial breakthrough came in 1784, when Henry Cort invented the 'puddling' process. This involves melting pig iron in a furnace, and burning off the carbon and other impurities in it: as the iron becomes purer it starts to solidify, and has to be worked into a 'bloom' of white-hot metal in the furnace. The 'bloom' is taken out of the furnace at white heat and worked (or 'wrought') with a hammer, then reheated in the furnace, taken out and hammered again, and this process repeated over and over again. When the bloom has been worked into a ductile state, it is run through a rolling mill at red heat to make rods, bars, 'angles' (bars bent into an L-shape), or plate. At the time this was a formidably difficult and expensive process, for it was right at the frontier of what was technically possible, but gradually the production techniques improved.

Why did they bother? Simply because wrought iron is a wonderful engineering material, with much higher tensile strength than cast. If you made a cast-iron beam and a wrought-iron beam of similar span and load-tested them both with progressively greater weights, eventually the cast-iron beam would break, suddenly and without warning. The wrought-iron beam would not: it would bend or distort in the middle, and it might bend a long way before it broke. Obviously, there are potential problems with a material this flexible: a structure like a roof or a bridge needs to have stiffness as well as flexibility. So the challenge for engineers, in using wrought iron, was to find the shapes and forms which would benefit from its tensile strength, while having enough stiffness to stand up under their own weight, resist wind pressure, carry loads, and generally do the job.

In 1841–5, Brunel had built his first large wrought-iron structure: the Hungerford Footbridge over the Thames in London. This was a suspension bridge with a central span 676 feet wide, carried on elegant brick towers in an Italianate style. Suspension bridge chain represented an ideal use for wrought iron: for the Hungerford Bridge, Brunel designed chains made up of four sets of links in parallel, each link 24 feet long and 7 inches deep. Though the Hungerford bridge had an impressive span, it was not especially innovative. Nevertheless, it must in some measure have made up for the disappointment of work stopping on the Clifton Bridge.

The design of suspension bridges was becoming well under-stood, but it was evident that they were too flexible to carry the heavy moving load of a railway train: a different approach was needed. It was becoming clear that designing with wrought iron didn't depend on the maximum size of one piece of iron (as was the case with cast-iron beams). Wrought-iron plates and angles could be riveted together to make beams or girders. Beams and bars could be combined to make trusses. The key was to find the strongest forms and shapes, and to understand how the forces would be transmitted through the structure.

Brunel seems to have started work in this area in 1847, the year of the Dee Bridge disaster, and also of the fire at the Uxbridge Road Bridge. He rebuilt the latter using wrought iron, so it may have had the distinction of being his first wrought-iron girder bridge as well as his first cast-iron bridge. Brunel designed a 'bowstring truss' for the Newport Viaduct after the original timber bridge was damaged by fire in 1848. He upped the scale, and designed a 200-foot bowstring truss for the bridge over the Thames on the GWR's little extension to Windsor, opened in 1849. He was also experimenting with designs for beams made of riveted wrought-iron plate, and came up with some curious but effective shapes with tubular top flanges, or top flanges that look like an upside-down C in section. A number of bridges with beams of these types are known to survive, like the 'swing bridge' at the Cumberland Basin in Bristol of 1848–9, or the road bridge at Balmoral of 1854–7 commissioned by the royal family. This fine bridge has a single span of 125 feet carried on two main girders, with transverse girders carrying a timber deck, a simple and elegant design which was, apparently, somewhat too simple to suit Queen Victoria's taste. Brunel designed many other wrought-iron girder bridges, but here again there are large gaps in our knowledge, though the likelihood is that most of them have been destroyed.

Brunel's career as a bridge designer culminated in his widest spans, those of the Chepstow Bridge over the Wye for the South Wales Railway (1850–52), and the Royal Albert Bridge over the Tamar at Saltash for the Cornwall Railway (1852–9). He was following in Robert Stephenson's wake somewhat, as his friend had just completed the two most ambitious and technically advanced iron bridges that the world had yet seen for the Chester & Holyhead Railway, one to carry it over the estuary of the Conway River at Conway (1846–8), and the Britannia Bridge over the Menai Straits (1848–50). Stephenson had developed huge 'tubular girders' made of wrought-iron plate, with help from the scientist Eaton Hodgkinson and the iron founder Sir William Fairbairn. They had found a way to take a railway across what had seemed unfeasibly wide gaps: a single span of 400 feet at Conway, and four spans of 460 feet each at the Menai Straits. Brunel was well aware of all this, having attended the 'floating' of the gigantic tubular girders for the Britannia Bridge to lend moral support to his friend.

When it came to designing his own bridges, though, his approach was totally different, and every bit as unprecedented as Stephenson's. At Chepstow he had to take his railway across the main river channel, 300 feet wide, and another 300 feet of river shore. He had initially considered building a big timber arch, but the Admiralty insisted that he provide a flat soffit 50 feet above the high-water mark for the ships. So instead, he crossed the river shore with three spans of 100 feet each, carried on simple wrought-iron plate girders, and for the main 300-foot span he devised a kind of truss so unlike anything else that no one has ever thought of a convenient name for it. It was a kind of suspension bridge, but whereas in a conventional suspension bridge the stresses are transferred to anchorage points in the ground at either end, at Chepstow the stresses were all contained within the structure, and everything was kept much more rigid to cope with the weight and vibration of railway trains. We do not know how Brunel arrived at this remarkable solution, but it was the dress rehearsal for his greatest bridge, at Saltash.

To link the Cornwall Railway to the rest of England the Hamoaze, the deep estuary of the River Tamar, had somehow to be crossed. In the early days this seemed so challenging that the company were thinking in terms of a ferry, but Brunel was confident that he could do it: at one stage, he seems to have been thinking in terms of a giant timber arch. The views of the Admiralty were paramount, and they demanded a clearance of 100 feet above high water. As it happened there was a large rock well below water level in the midstream, and in 1848 Brunel designed an iron cylinder, 85 feet long, which could be floated out, sunk onto the rock and pumped out. From the cylinder, 175 trial borings were made to map the rock's surface, establishing that it could be used as the base for a central pier. Brunel produced a design for a bridge with two great spans of 465 feet, but the Cornwall Railway's restricted finances would not bear this, and in 1852 he produced a reduced design for a single track, with the main spans reduced to 455 feet. For these, Brunel perfected the concept developed at Chepstow. It might be described as a 'closed' suspension bridge: indeed, the unused chains made back in 1843 for his Clifton Bridge were bought and incorporated into it, though a lot more needed to be made. The deck is kept rigid by a lot of cross-bracing, and the whole thing is braced by the huge cylindrical top tube. As at Chepstow, the stresses are all contained within the structure. The whole bridge, including its approach viaducts, would be 2,200 feet long. Brunel was paid £5,000 for his design, which he accepted in shares in the Cornwall Railway Company.

C.J. Mare of Blackwall, a shipbuilder who specialised in iron construction, offered to build this huge structure for £167,000. Mare had been the main contractor for Stephenson's Britannia

Bridge: no better preparation could have been envisaged, but unfortunately on this occasion he had seriously underestimated his bid. The most complicated part of the whole project involved building the central pier off the submerged rock, about 80 feet below water level. To do this, Brunel devised a huge cylindrical iron caisson, which was held between large pontoons, and lowered into place. The air was pressurised to help keep the water out, and teams of men worked in this sweltering atmosphere, hacking away at the rock and starting to lay the granite foundations within the great cylinder. Meanwhile, the viaducts at either end started to rise, and the first of the bridge's main trusses began to take shape on the north (Devon) shore. In 1855, with the work at roughly this point, the contractor went bankrupt.

Brunel and his team, led by his assistant R. P. Brereton, had immense difficulties getting the work back on track with directly employed labour. In 1857 the first truss was completed and load tested, and on 1 September it was floated out on great pontoons into position. This was an immensely complex operation, requiring great precision, in which 500 men were involved. Brunel planned it in meticulous detail, drawing on his experiences of attending Stephenson's operations at the Menai Straits and performing similar tasks for his own Chepstow Bridge. Once the vast truss was in place, resting on the pier bases, hydraulic jacks were fitted under each end. The huge structure was gradually lifted, three feet at a time, while the piers were built up underneath it. Ten months later it had reached its final position. The whole operation then had to be repeated for the second truss, which was floated out on 10 July 1858. The total cost had been £225,000, as compared to £601,865 for the Britannia Bridge.

The Royal Albert Bridge was inaugurated by the Prince Consort in a triumphant opening ceremony on 2 May 1859, but sadly Brunel was unable to be there: he was still travelling on the Continent, for the sake of his declining health. Shortly after returning to England, he managed to visit. A special train drew a waggon slowly across the bridge: on the waggon was a couch, and on the couch lay the designer of this marvel. It was the only time that he saw it complete.

6

The Three Great Ships

In October 1835, Brunel was attending a meeting of the Great Western Railway's directors at Radley's Hotel in Blackfriars, London. One of the more nervous spirits present expressed concern at the length of the proposed main line to Bristol, and Brunel is said to have riposted: 'Why not make it longer, and have a steamboat go from Bristol to New York, and call it the Great Western'. It is the kind of story which sounds as if it is probably made up or exaggerated, but actually it seems to be perfectly true. Furthermore this was, quite literally, the origin of the Great Western Steamship Company, and of a revolutionary advance in ship design.

Back in 1819, as a schoolboy in Hove, the young Isambard had written to his mother that he had 'been making half a dozen boats lately, till I've worn my hands to pieces'. There is little or no evidence that Brunel had any more practical experience of shipbuilding than these childhood pursuits, and it does seem surprising that in 1835, while furiously busy with the design of his railway, he should have found time to think about this completely different subject. And of course, he did a lot more than think about ship design: in a few years he mastered it, and transformed it.

In 1835 ship design was ripe for a revolution: a lot of new ideas were emerging, waiting for someone to put them together. Shipbuilding had always been a rather enclosed world, more craft-based than science-based. It lived and worked according to its own customs and traditions, and the scientific advances of the 17th and 18th centuries had not made nearly as much impression on it as one might expect. So perhaps it isn't a paradox that it took someone from outside this enclosed world, who had not been indoctrinated in its prejudices and outlook, to make the intellectual leaps that were needed.

It would be wrong, though, to belittle the achievements of this old world: the design of timber ships had evolved slowly over many centuries, but with ultimately spectacular results. Very large timber ships were prone to weakness, from the flexible nature of their material. Britain's Royal Dockyards devoted their best efforts to achieving both size and strength: Nelson's HMS *Victory*, at over 2,200 tons, was for its time a very large ship of remarkably robust construction. A rather commoner type was represented by the passenger or packet ships, mostly American owned, which dominated the North Atlantic run in the years after Waterloo: typically about 180 feet long and up to around 1,000 tons, they were fast and reliable.

The design of masts, sails and rigging were all improving too: the tea trade to China and the wool trade to Australia were becoming more competitive, and speed was becoming more of an issue. It is important, when thinking about the revolution in iron-built, steam-powered ships that Brunel did so much to bring about, to bear in mind that sailing ships still had a vital role to play, and only reached their ultimate point of development after his death: the *Cutty Sark* wasn't launched until 1869. The best sailing ship in the world, though, was still at the mercy of the wind, the weather and the currents: so the Black Ball Line, for example, one of the most efficient of the companies doing the Liverpool to New York run with a fleet of 500-ton sailing packets, in its first nine years of service (1816–25) averaged 23 days travelling eastwards to Britain, but 40 days going west to the United States.

The biggest new ideas in ship design in the early 19th century were about using iron as a hull material, and about using steam power to drive the ship. Brunel was not absolutely a pioneer in these areas, but his contribution in developing others' ideas was of immense importance. Where he did make an absolutely fundamental contribution was to do with the optimum size of a ship: the relationship between the size of the hull, the size of engine needed to drive it, the volume of fuel required to power it, the number of days' worth of fuel that a ship of given size could carry, and the resistance of the sea that the ship had to push against. Brunel took the received wisdom of the age on these subjects, and he blew it apart with an inimitable blend of mathematics and instinct.

To take steam power first. Like many advances in technology it was pioneered separately in at least two places. The very first viable steamship was probably the *Charlotte Dundas*, a tugboat with a stern paddle wheel, launched on the Clyde in 1801. In 1807 the American Robert Fulton launched his *Clermont* on the

Hudson River. In 1812 Henry Bell launched the *Comet*, the first steamship to operate a commercial ferry service, on the Clyde and then the Firth of Forth. Then in 1814 Marc Brunel, not one to be far behind the leaders where mechanical invention was concerned, launched his steam boat, the *Regent*, which ran a successful ferry service between London and Margate. There was certainly a spirit of competition in the air, and ships with steam engines actually crossed the Atlantic: the American *Savannah* in 1819, and the Dutch *Curaçao* in 1824. However, it is not merely a case of British sour grapes to deny these vessels the honour of having made the first steam-powered crossings, for the fact is that they were medium-sized sailing ships, with little engines and paddles for use when there was no wind and the sea was flat: the *Savannah*'s boilers were fired up for just 84 hours out of a 29-day crossing, while the *Curaçao*'s were fired for 12 days out of 28.

Herein lay the nub of the problem. Up to 1835, the conventional wisdom had it that steamships were really only viable for short runs. Neither the *Savannah* nor the *Curaçao* could have held enough coal to power them across the Atlantic unaided (not even if they hadn't carried anything else). It was assumed that the coal consumed by a steamship, and thus the weight of coal it needed to carry, would increase in proportion with the size of the ship, as measured by its displacement (the weight of the water displaced by the hull). So if no small ship could carry enough coal to cross the Atlantic, it followed that no big ship could either. Almost everyone, including Marc Brunel, seems to have accepted this as a fundamental obstacle. At some point around 1835, we do not know quite when or how, his son realised that the fundamental obstacle was really a fundamental mistake. The energy, whether from wind or steam, which is needed to drive a ship through the water depends not so much on the vessel's weight (the point about ships being that they are buoyant!) or even its displacement, as on the resistance – the weight of the water that it has to push against. In other words, the critical factors are the surface area of the hull that is in contact with the water, and its shape – and a 2,000-ton ship does not have anything like twice the surface area of a 1,000-ton ship. As a simple demonstration of this, imagine a cube with sides one foot square: its volume is one cubic foot and its surface area is six square feet. Now picture a cube with two-foot sides (that is, measuring four square feet): it has eight times the volume (eight cubic feet), but only four times the surface area (24 square feet). The area increases as a square, but the volume increases as a cube. Brunel realised that the cube-square law was the key to the whole question. The bigger the ship, the more favourable the energy-to-weight equation would be.

This brings us to October 1835, and dinner at Radley's Hotel. After dinner, Brunel was buttonholed by one of the most lively and interesting of the GWR directors, Thomas Guppy. He was an engineer and a sugar refiner, from one of Bristol's richest merchant families. Brunel might have intended his challenge as a dinner-table joke, but to Guppy it seemed an exciting proposition. Why not, indeed! Guppy and Brunel talked late into the night, and then made contact with a number of colleagues including Captain Christopher Claxton, a half-pay naval officer who was the Quay Warden of Bristol Docks, and William Patterson, who was Bristol's most respected shipbuilder. Three more GWR directors came on board; within a matter of weeks a handwritten prospectus was being circulated around a few other rich and daring Bristolians; and on 3 March 1836 the Great Western Steamship Company held its first public meeting. This was how business got done then.

The new company came to legal life on 2 June: a good deal of capital had already been raised, and later the same month a keel 205 feet long (the longest keel in the world, in fact), was laid at

William Patterson's shipyard on the Floating Harbour. A Building Committee of Brunel, Guppy and Claxton were to meet Patterson once a week to control the construction: Brunel was giving his services free. The *Great Western* was going to be a very large ship for its time, 236 feet long overall, of 1,340 tons weight and 2,300 tons displacement, constructed of oak with a copper-sheathed hull and very strongly framed following the ideas of Sir Robert Seppings, Surveyor to the Royal Navy. The design in detail of the hull and its four schooner-rigged masts probably owed more to Seppings' influence and Patterson's experience than to Brunel, who had not actually built a ship before.

His particular contribution was in the overall conception, and in the design of the pair of engines, which would power twin paddle wheels 28 feet in diameter. To build them Brunel chose the firm of Maudslay, Son & Field in Lambeth – the firm that had worked for his father so often. What Brunel specified, and Maudslay designed in detail and built, was termed a side-lever engine – a little like a beam engine, but with the beam (which links the steam-piston to the connecting rod which turns the paddle wheels) placed low down to one side, hence the name. In fact it was a pair of engines, each with a cylinder 70 inches in diameter, placed side by side, with their connecting rods linked to a single paddle wheel shaft, acting in alternation. The two sides had a theoretical combined horsepower of 750, but in practice the combined nominal horsepower was about 450: it was, by a considerable margin, the biggest marine engine that had ever been built.

So from 1836 into 1837, the hull took shape in Patterson's yard, and the engines were under construction in Lambeth, and Brunel looked in at both places when he had the opportunity. Halfway through construction, Brunel was involved in a public dispute with one of the great pundits of the day, the wonderfully named Dr Dionysius Lardner. Dr Lardner was actually a scientist of some substance, but he had an unfortunate tendency to set himself up as a public authority on all scientific and technological matters, and today he is principally remembered for those of his judgements which came most spectacularly unstuck. Like when, in August 1836, he came to address the British Association for the Advancement of Science in Bristol. Dr Lardner informed an awed audience that the water resistance encountered by a ship was directly proportional to its displacement, not the surface area in contact. From here, he proceeded to demonstrate that a steamship of 2,000 tons would require eight times the horsepower to maintain a given speed than one of 1,000 tons, and that the longest voyage that any ship could carry coal for was 2,500 miles. He concluded impressively that:

> Making a voyage (i.e. by steam) directly from New York to Liverpool was perfectly chimerical, and they might as well talk of making a voyage from New York or Liverpool to the moon.

Dr Lardner's views, of course, were more or less the opposite of the truth and Brunel, who was in the audience, rose to his feet to try and prove this. The exchange is not recorded, but Brunel apparently did not score a hit. It is worth remembering Dr Lardner, to remind ourselves of the originality of Brunel's thinking, and the courage and confidence that his backers needed when faced with criticism from so apparently authoritative a source.

On 19 July 1837, regardless of Dr Lardner's opinions, the *Great Western* was launched, and on 18 August she set sail for London to receive her engines. She apparently handled very easily and well, and would doubtless have been a success as a sailing ship. The big ship berthed in the East India Dock, and over the next six months carts trundled through the crowded streets from Maudslay's works in Lambeth to Blackwall, carrying the components of her engines. In March 1838 all was ready, and the *Great Western* had four days of engine trials, managing an average speed of 11 knots very comfortably. She was due to return to Bristol in April and pick up passengers and cargo for her maiden voyage to New York – the first continuous crossing of the Atlantic by steam.

However, the North Atlantic trade was a very competitive business, and other parties were beginning to realise that Brunel was right and Lardner was wrong. By the time the *Great Western* had been fitted out, companies from both London and Liverpool were converting existing ships to compete with her. The London company was in the lead, having chartered a little steamer called the *Sirius*, of 703 tons and 320 horsepower, which had recently been built for the Irish run. In late March, while the *Great Western* was still testing her engines, the *Sirius* set out from London with 22 passengers: on 4 April she took on coal at Cork and set off for New York, in a deliberate bid to beat the Bristolians. As a venture it was brave to the point of rashness, and by rights the *Great Western* should have won even given the *Sirius*' head-start, but for an accident on her way back to Bristol.

The *Great Western* slipped her moorings early on 31 March. Brunel was on board, and his ship seemed to be performing beautifully, but at about noon, with the ship sailing down the Thames estuary, flames and smoke were seen pouring from the engine room. The lagging around the boiler had been carried up too high around the flue and had got hot and ignited. The Captain, Lieutenant Hosken, put his ship aground on the soft mud and the fire was quickly brought under control, but Brunel, attempting to descend a ladder into the engine-room to see what was going on, stepped through a burnt rung and fell 20 feet. He landed on top of his friend Captain Claxton, and fell on the flooded engine room floor. Claxton, fortunately, was uninjured, and pulled the unconscious figure out to find that it was Brunel, whom he had almost certainly saved from drowning. Brunel was quite badly injured, but this did not prevent him from dictating a long memo about the well-being of the ship to Claxton later the same day.

All sorts of rumours about the *Great Western* had reached Bristol by the time the ship arrived there on 2 April, and most of the passengers for the scheduled maiden voyage had cancelled their reservations in panic. So it was with full coal bunkers but with a mere seven passengers that the *Great Western* set out, in pursuit of the *Sirius*, on 7 April 1838. She did not need to stop at Cork to refuel, and she was catching up every day. Despite some heavy weather, rough enough to carry away part of the fore topmast, the *Great Western* made the crossing in 17 days, coming in sight of New York around noon on 23 April. Proudly moored there was the *Sirius* which, despite her several days' head-start, had arrived (and run aground) the previous evening, with precious little coal left in her holds: the *Great Western*, on the other hand, still had 200 tons left. The race between the ships had electrified New York and crowds of visitors flocked to see both. The two ships roughly repeated their performances on the return journey, bearing in mind the more favourable currents, the *Great Western* taking 14 days and the *Sirius* 18 days. The advantage of steam power over sail could not have been demonstrated more plainly, and the *Great Western* went into regular and profitable service for her owners, making 67 crossings in eight years. Dr Lardner's reaction does not seem to be recorded.

The *Great Western*'s success was such that Brunel and the company were almost immediately thinking of their next ship.

The same building committee, of Brunel, Guppy and Claxton, started to develop their ideas, and at first they were thinking of a large wooden ship with paddle wheels – really a bigger version of the *Great Western* but by late 1838 their thoughts were turning to the idea of iron construction. At this point, by chance, an iron-hulled paddle steamer called the *Rainbow* docked in Bristol. Brunel was interested, and asked Claxton and Patterson to sail to Antwerp in the ship, observing her performance.

An iron ship meant a ship with a framing of wrought-iron bars and beams, clad with wrought-iron plates riveted together. So the whole idea only became possible once wrought iron could be produced on a large scale, and the very first iron vessel, a 70-foot-long canal barge, had been made by the iron founder John Wilkinson in 1787, just three years after Henry Cort's invention of the puddling furnace. The idea initially provoked a lot of scepticism, but by the 1820s medium-sized ocean-going iron ships were being produced on the Clyde and the Mersey. It was becoming clear that an iron hull only had about 70 per cent of the weight of an equivalent timber hull and was drier and thinner (thus gaining more usable hull space). Between September 1838 and June 1839, Brunel and his colleagues produced six draft designs in succession. The first was for a wooden ship 236 feet long and weighing 1,340 tons; the last was for an iron ship 322 feet and weighing 3,675 tons. It was a period of intensive design development culminating in the largest and most innovative hull design the world had ever seen, and it is important to remember that Brunel was doing this during the most critical and stressful phase of building the Great Western Railway. His hull design had a two-skinned cellular construction along its bottom, and a very strongly constructed iron deck on top. It had six watertight compartments running across the hull, and two longitudinal bulkheads, running the length of the ship.

Brunel's hull can be likened to a great box girder, anticipating the work of Robert Stephenson and Sir William Fairbairn on box-girder bridges, and this gave the ship great longitudinal strength. The keel was laid in Patterson's yard at Bristol on 19 July 1839, with the Great Western Steamship Company using his facilities but acting as their own contractors.

There was a protracted wrangle over the design and manufacture of the engines. Brunel wanted Maudslay, Son & Field again, but the company, against his advice, preferred a lower bid from a young engineer called Francis Humphrys. The great iron hull would require a much larger engine than anything yet produced, and Brunel's concerns were soon shown to be justified, for by the end of the year Humphrys was floundering, having found, among other problems, that there was no hammer in the world big enough to forge the main drive shaft for the paddles. He wrote to his friend James Nasmyth, to solicit his help, and the direct result was Nasmyth's invention of his steam hammer, one of the key innovations behind Victorian heavy industry.

In May 1840 fate took another turn, with the arrival of another experimental vessel, the *Archimedes*, in Bristol. This was the brainchild of a gentleman engineer, Francis Pettit Smith, and it was the world's first working propeller-driven ship. Brunel was immediately interested. Thomas Guppy was interested too, and took a trip to Liverpool on her. When he reported back, the directors were so impressed that they ordered work on the paddle engines for their new steamer to stop, and chartered the *Archimedes* for six months of trial voyages.

Brunel quickly realised that a propeller, being fully immersed, represents a much more efficient use of energy. In December 1840 he reported to the board, recommending that their new ship, the largest that had ever been built, should be solely propeller-driven. The decision seems to have been a fatal

blow for Francis Humphrys, already suffering severe strain as a
result of his attempt to build the world's largest marine engine
for an inadequate tender price. Now he was ordered to stop
work, and he seems to have died from the strain. His friend
Nasmyth wrote:

> Mr Humphrys was a man of the most sensitive and sanguine
> constitution of mind. The labour and anxiety which he had
> already undergone, and perhaps the disappointment of his
> hopes, proved too much for him and a brain fever carried him
> off after a few days' illness.

Poor Humphrys was a victim of his own over-optimism, but also
of Brunel's insatiable intellectual curiosity and perfectionism.
So now Brunel was left with no engine, and no design for one.
Only one propeller-driven ship had ever been built, and there
was precious little data to go on. The directors agreed that their
new ship could wait while Brunel and Pettit Smith investigated.
It seems an extraordinary decision for any commercial
organisation to take: a lot of money was tied up in that big iron
hull. In the event, it was over two years before work resumed on
the ship which became known as the *Great Britain*.

The Royal Navy, or rather a few adventurous individuals, in
particular Captain Edward Parry who controlled its steamship
department, were also becoming interested. After a lot of
official opposition and delay, Brunel and Pettit Smith were
commissioned to develop designs for a propeller-driven ship and
undertake trials. In 1842 work began on an 800-ton sloop, the
Rattler, with engines by Maudslay: she was launched in April
1843, and trial voyages were undertaken with a succession of
different propellers to find the best shape. The *Rattler*'s most
famous moment came in April 1845, when she was matched
against a similarly-sized paddle-driven sloop, the *Alecto*, for a

tug-of-war: with the ships facing in opposite directions, tied stern-to-stern and both operating at full power, the *Rattler* towed the *Alecto* backwards at over two knots. Game, set and match to the screw propeller.

By this time, the *Great Britain* was finished and in service. Brunel used the Admiralty data to design a six-bladed propeller 15 feet in diameter: his design was so good that modern propellers are only about 5 per cent more efficient. With the unfortunate Francis Humphrys gone, Brunel designed the great 1,500 horsepower engines himself, and they were manufactured on site by the company. The *Great Britain* was launched by the Prince Consort in July 1843, and moved out of the dry dock into the Floating Harbour for fitting out. Getting her out of the Floating Harbour, however, involved difficulties which verged on the ludicrous. The Great Western Steamship Company had built this very large ship, 322 feet long and up to 51 feet in breadth, as they had received firm assurances from the Bristol Dock Company that the locks between the Floating Harbour and the Avon were about to be widened. The Dock Company had once again demonstrated its remarkable capacity for letting people down and nothing had been done. The *Great Britain* almost got jammed in the lock on the first attempt to get it out, and Brunel had to get the Dock Company's permission to remove some of the stonework, in order to release his creation into the River Avon on 12 December 1844. She then had to sail to London to complete her rather protracted fitting-out. It was no wonder that Liverpool was winning the battle of the Atlantic.

The *Great Britain*, with a displacement of 3,675 tons (as compared to 2,300 for the *Great Western*) was the largest ship afloat. With her unprecedented size, the highly innovative design of her iron hull, the largest engines that had ever been built, and her superbly efficient screw propeller, she was by far the most technically advanced ship that had ever been built. She is arguably the single most important vessel, in terms of ship design, in history. On her maiden voyage in August 1845 she made the crossing to New York in 14 days, and returned in 15. The ship was a technical triumph, but the Great Western Steamship Company was in poor financial health, and furthermore, as the circumstances of her launch had demonstrated, the *Great Britain* was just too big to be worked out of Bristol, so she was based in the rival port of Liverpool. Departing for New York in September 1846, the ship went aground on a reef off Dundrum in Ulster, the captain having been misled by an error in his chart. The crew and passengers were taken off, and to Brunel's absolute fury, there his great ship stayed, for almost a year. The Company reacted with stunned torpor, and if it hadn't been for their engineer's determination, the *Great Britain* might well have been written off. At his urging, a protective barrier of wood was built to preserve the ship from the battering waves, the damage to the hull repaired, and the *Great Britain* was successfully refloated in August 1847: it was a testimony to the strength and merit of Brunel's hull design. The Great Western Steamship Company, though, succumbed to the financial strain, and their two ships were sold. It was the end for the vision that Brunel had hinted at twelve years earlier at Radley's Hotel, but his ships' place in history was already assured.

The construction of his third ship, the *Great Eastern*, dominated the last six years of Brunel's life: it generated great controversy at the time, it continues to generate controversy among historians to this day, and it has often been blamed for causing Brunel's death. There is a huge volume of documentary evidence, but it is incomplete: most of the personal and business papers of the ship's builder, John Scott Russell, are missing. It is a strange story, many aspects of it don't seem to add up, and its complexities can only be hinted at here.

The first thing to bear in mind is that from the outset this was Brunel's idea: no one ever asked him to design the world's largest ship. It began in 1851, when the Australian Mail Steam Company consulted him about designs for ships which would only need to take on coal once, at the Cape of Good Hope. Brunel produced a specification for iron steamships with a displacement of 5,000 to 6,000 tons, which the company considered too ambitious. Instead they commissioned a pair of rather smaller ships, the *Adelaide* and *Victoria*, from the eminent contractor John Scott Russell, which could still carry enough coal to fulfil this basic criterion. It was becoming clear that maintaining coaling stations in distant ports was a difficult and expensive business, and Brunel started thinking about how big a ship would need to be to carry its own fuel for a journey to the Far East, and even more ambitiously, to carry its own fuel for the return trip. One day in 1852, he worked out several pages of calculations in one of his sketchbooks, by the end of which he was envisaging a ship over 600 feet long, with bunker space for over 10,000 tons of coal, and a displacement of over 21,000 tons. From then on visions of giant ships and pages of calculations fill the sketchbooks. By the time the design was finalised, late in 1853, the ship's dimensions had risen to 692 feet long by 83 feet broad, weighing 18,915 tons and displacing 27,000 tons, with room for 4,000 passengers and 3,000 tons of cargo. It would have a single propeller providing about 60 per cent of the motive power, and paddle wheels to provide the other 40 per cent. It would be six times the size of his own *Great Britain* (322 feet long and displacing 3,675 tons), which had itself been the biggest ship in the world at the time it was launched.

Was there really the demand for such a monster? Brunel was convinced that the demand would appear once the ship was built, and he approached the recently formed Eastern Steam

Navigation Company, which had been founded to bid for the mail contracts to the Far East, but had lost to the Peninsular & Oriental Company, and seems to have been looking for a way forward. Brunel must have dazzled them with his vision, for in July 1852 he was appointed as their engineer. He and a number of friends, led by the banker and ironmaster Charles Geach, then set about reconstructing the company. For the rest of 1852 and through 1853, Brunel and Geach were reshaping the ESNC's board and vigorously selling shares, using the credit and the contacts Brunel had made in his 20-year career. By 1854 the ESNC was a very different company from the one set up in 1851: it had become a vehicle for the construction of Brunel's great ship. He had never before been so deeply committed to a project, financially and morally as well as intellectually and practically.

Even at this point, several questions thrust themselves forward. The ESNC's board was full of hard-nosed businessmen: why did they, and Brunel, stake the company on the building of a single monster ship of unprecedented size and design, with all the concentration of risk that this entailed? Did they think about how many ports could actually accommodate this giant, and what effect that would have on their business? Had they investigated the demand for cargo space on this vast scale, in either direction? Brunel's reports include a few ideas, with very few figures, about the demand side: is this all there was? We do not know the answers, and are obliged to move on to the next set of questions, which relate to construction and cost.

In 1852, Brunel had tentatively estimated the cost of the great ship at £500,000: its scale, and his years of experience, must surely have taught him caution about estimating. In May 1853 tenders were invited for building the ship: three companies, including John Scott Russell's, tendered for building the engines, but only Scott Russell seems to have entered a tender for actually building the ship. He offered to build this giant for £377,200, made up of £275,200 for the hull, £42,000 for the paddle engines and boilers, and another £60,000 for the screw engines and boilers: the latter were to be subcontracted to James Watt & Company in Birmingham. Scott Russell's tender proved to be a disastrous underestimate but there was no other bidder, and Brunel accepted it, telling the directors that he found the figures 'highly satisfactory'. A detailed contract was let, specifying among other things that the ship was to be built in a dock, despite the fact that there was no dry dock in the world anywhere near big enough for the purpose. Scott Russell apparently proposed that he would build such a dock, 700 feet long and 100 feet wide, for £10,000: this seems a particularly glaring underestimate.

Scott Russell is an interesting, enigmatic personality. He was of humble Scots origins, but had risen by talent and a good education, through the universities of Glasgow and Edinburgh, to become an academic and a practising mechanical engineer. He involved himself in ship design, carrying out some of the first serious experiments on the relationship between hull shape and a ship's performance: though his 'wave-line' theory was later shown to be flawed, he deserves to be remembered as a pioneer in this area. In 1844 he had moved to London as a consulting engineer, and in 1847 he joined a partnership which was formed to buy a large shipyard on the Isle of Dogs from William Fairbairn. He was also deeply involved in the Society of Arts, and in the initiative, formed there, which developed into the Great Exhibition of 1851. So Scott Russell was a distinguished man: by 1853 he had been running a large and apparently successful shipyard for some years, and he was one of the most experienced builders of iron ships in the world. We have no idea how he arrived at his disastrously low figure for building Brunel's great ship: indeed, he offered to build the hull for

£258,000 if the ESNC commissioned him to build the second sister ship that they were envisaging. It is possible, given what followed, that his business was already suffering cash-flow problems in 1853 and that he 'bought' the contract, not realising that no one else was tendering for it and thinking that the regular payments made by the ESNC would help him recover, but this is mere speculation.

In 1854, Scott Russell leased the Napier Yard next door to his, which had become available, so as to have sufficient room. It had become clear that neither he nor the ESNC could afford to build a dock big enough in which to build Brunel's giant ship. Scott Russell proposed to build it end-on to the river, on a sloping launching way, but Brunel rejected the idea on a number of grounds, including the great height of the higher (bow) end in such an arrangement. So they decided that the ship would be built on timber launching ways: a series of massive beams set on piles driven into the muddy foreshore. This committed them to a sideways launch, but it wasn't until well into the construction process that either Brunel or Scott Russell seems to have started grappling with the implications of this decision.

The first stage of building the *Leviathan* (as it was originally going to be called) lasted from early 1854 until February 1856, when Scott Russell became insolvent and his creditors took over his business. It is an appallingly complicated story, and it is unlikely that it will ever be reconstructed in full, but a number of points can be made. First, that Scott Russell's yard was making a superb job of executing this vast and unprecedented design given the equipment and materials at their disposal: no one has ever cast doubt on the quality of the construction. Second, Brunel did make numerous changes to the design, which would have increased the cost. Third, though it is harder to be sure about this, Scott Russell seems to have been accepting some of the payment in shares in the ESNC: as the company's

Brunel's office at 17 Duke Street, to which he moved from his previous office in number 18, in 1849. This photograph, which was probably taken shortly after Brunel's death in 1859, shows his desk with its in- and out-trays, and a portrait of Marc Brunel over the chimneypiece. The window wall is filled by a long desk for rolling out (or producing) drawings.

The Clifton Bridge under construction, with a footway slung between the towers on which the first of the chains was to be assembled.

A chromolithograph of the SS *Great Eastern* afloat by T.G. Dutton. Brunel never lived to see his 'great babe' at sea.

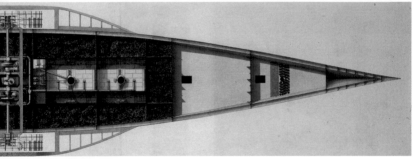

The longitudinal plan and section of the *Great Eastern*. At 692 feet long it would be over 40 years before a longer ship was built. The cross-section shows the two engine rooms and the machinery required to turn the screw propeller and the side paddle wheels. The bottom was designed to be strong and stable enough to be beached for repairs or maintenance as the *Great Eastern* was too big to fit in any of the world's dry-docks.

The Crystal Palace in Hyde Park, which in 1851 housed the Great Exhibition: the most revolutionary building of the 19th century anywhere in the world. Paxton conceived it, Sir Charles Fox made the design work, and Fox, Henderson & Company constructed this vast structure in about five months, for £89,950. Brunel was involved throughout as a member of the Building Committee.

The Clifton Bridge as completed, with the fine Georgian houses of Clifton stretching off to the right, and a low tide on the River Avon. The entrance locks to the Cumberland Basin and the Floating Harbour are just out of the picture, to the right.

The steel frame for Tower Bridge under construction *c.* 1890.

An engraving of Paddington Station from the *Illustrated London News*, showing the great train-shed with its cross-transepts and Matthew Digby Wyatt's decorative end-glazing.

Brunel's earliest surviving iron bridge, running over a canal just outside Paddington Station. Long forgotten and unrecognised, it was due to be demolished as part of a scheme for a major new road bridge and was rediscovered, in the nick of time, in 2003. The bridge is seen in the process of being dismantled for reconstruction on a nearby site.

financial position worsened, the shares fell in value, to the point of being untradable. When Scott Russell's bankers closed his business down, most of the contract price for the hull had been paid, but only about half of it had been built (again, the evidence is unclear). Some historians have laid the blame on Scott Russell, arguing that he had been dishonest and fraudulent, but it is not necessary to believe this to explain the débâcle (for which there were plenty of alternative causes), nor does it seem very plausible.

After a prolonged bout of wrangling, the ESNC took over the Napier Yard itself and work resumed on the great ship. More capital had to be raised, and Brunel spent much more time at Millwall, urging the work forward. In the autumn of 1857 the ship was almost ready for launching. The full implications of building it on the Thames foreshore, just above the high-water mark, now became clear. Scott Russell had favoured what he called a 'free launch', meaning that the ship would be slid down timber launching ways, with a slope of about 1 in 12: the launching ways would be greased, and the ship would slide down them in its timber cradle without restraint, in the traditional manner. Brunel thought this dangerous. Also, he seems to have thought that the timber cradles would bind against the timber launching ways. Brunel wanted to devise a controlled launch. Late in 1856 he took the fateful decision to have iron plates fixed to the underside of the launching cradles, and to have iron rails fixed to the launching ways.

By the beginning of November 1857 the great hull was ready, and Brunel's launching system was about to be put to the test. He had planned the operation to the last detail. Chains, attached to the launching cradles, were linked to great steam-powered winches on barges in the Thames. These would pull, and big hydraulic presses on the landward side of the ship would push: the iron cradles would slide slowly on their iron-plated undersides down the iron rails of the launching ways. Once the ship started to slide, her progress would be checked by the weight of huge chains wound onto drums. The great ship would be lowered to the low-water mark, and wait to be floated off on the high tide. That, at any rate, was the idea.

Brunel's enormous ship, which was informally becoming known as the *Great Eastern*, was attracting intense interest from the press and the public, and the directors of the company, desperate to raise funds, had sold great numbers of tickets for the launch. To Brunel's horror, he found that he was going to have to carry out this supremely difficult operation in front of a vast audience. The river, too, was full of spectators in small craft. Brunel gave the signal, the winches laboured for ten minutes, the great hull shuddered, then suddenly the bow end moved about three feet. The crew of the stern checking drum let their attention wander and its handle spun out of control, throwing one of the labourers into the air, as the stern of the ship shot forward by four feet. The labourer was crushed by flying chains and died of his injuries soon after. A further attempt that afternoon failed completely. The whole fiasco was witnessed by an immense crowd. What had gone wrong? We cannot be quite sure, but Brunel may have made a serious error in devising a system based on the use of iron plates running over iron rails, instead of relying on well-greased timber as Scott Russell had proposed. Loaded with the vast weight of the *Great Eastern*, the iron-plated launching cradles had not run smoothly; they had done the opposite.

It took another two months to get the *Great Eastern* into the water. Brunel had more hydraulic presses brought down: they strained and pushed away, and by 30 November the ship had moved about 33 feet. A host of correspondents wrote in with advice, most of it useless. Much more helpfully, Robert Stephenson came to visit. His advice was simple: 'more power'.

So Brunel's assistants scoured the country for more hydraulic plant. They pushed and heaved, and at last on 31 January 1858, the *Great Eastern* floated.

Her construction had been immensely stressful and difficult throughout, though the awful saga of the launch must have been the worst part yet, and there was more to come. The ship had cost £600,000 and counting, the launch had cost £120,000, and another £200,000 was still needed to install the engines and fit her out, and the Eastern Steam Navigation Company were unable to raise this. So, after several months more delay, a new company, the Great Ship Company, was formed and bought the incomplete vessel from the ESNC for £165,000, and the latter company went into liquidation with huge losses. Brunel had been working for no salary since Scott Russell's bankruptcy, and paying his assistants out of his own pocket. Besides this, whatever Brunel had invested in the ESNC, and it was a lot, he, like all the other shareholders, must have lost it all.

Brunel spent the winter of 1858 in the Mediterranean, on his doctors' orders, and meanwhile the new company was preparing to fit out the *Great Eastern*. John Scott Russell had revived his business and, surprising as it might seem, he entered a tender for its completion, which the Great Ship Company accepted. Work resumed, in an atmosphere of some tension, and by the summer of 1859 the services of arbitrators were needed, but nevertheless the ship was nearing completion: the paddle engines received their first trial in July and the screw engines on 1 August. Brunel, by now very seriously ill, visited the ship as often as he could. On 5 August, Scott Russell held a banquet on board, though Brunel was too ill to attend. The date of the maiden voyage, around the coast to Holyhead, was fixed for 3 September. Brunel was anxious to be on board and on 2 September he visited the ship again. He was photographed, looking sadly thin and frail: it is the last known photograph of

him. A couple of hours later he collapsed on board the ship and
was taken home.

On 7 September, the *Great Eastern* slipped her moorings and
headed down the Thames. The Great Ship Company was
showing signs of dividing into warring factions and the lines of
command on the ship were not as clear as they might have been.
Brunel was anxiously awaiting news of his 'great babe' on his
sickbed at Duke Street. Towards 6 p.m. on 8 September, the
ship, standing off Dungeness, was shaken by a terrific explosion:
the forward funnel shot into the air. Five stokers were killed and
several more seriously injured. It turned out that a stopcock on
the water pre-heater, wrapped around the forward funnel, had
been accidentally left shut. The pressure had built up without
anyone knowing. The ship was not actually very seriously
damaged, but the loss of life was tragic, and it seemed to
confirm her reputation as an unlucky ship. Brunel was told of
the accident on 10 September. By this time the end was very
near anyway: we cannot say if this dreadful news hastened it. He
died on 15 September 1859.

The *Great Eastern* was a masterpiece of design. The hull
design, with its double skin, its transverse bulkheads and its
tremendous longitudinal strength, embodied much of the
future of shipbuilding. The combination of paddles and
propeller gave the ship remarkable manoeuvrability for its size,
though by later standards it would have seemed underpowered.
The structure was so strongly built that it took two years to
break up. The fitting-out and decoration were splendid, like one
of the grandest hotels of the age. Above all, she was very, very
large: it was to be 49 years before another ship, the Cunard liner
Lusitania, outstripped her in size. Yet from almost every point of
view, the ship was too big, too far ahead of her time.

The *Great Eastern* never operated on the Far East routes for
which she was designed, and lost money on both passengers and

cargo. She suffered dreadful damage in a great storm in September 1861 and was repaired at great cost, only to run aground off the American coast in August 1862. Brunel's superb design survived both these trials, but between them they sank the Great Ship Company. The only profitable use that was ever found for her was in laying sub-oceanic cables, where at last her gigantic holds and superb manoeuvrability came into their own. Everyone else lost money, including the shipbreakers who destroyed her.

Brunel's genius had conceived her, his charisma had foisted this vision onto his dazzled contemporaries, including Scott Russell, and lured their money out of their pockets. His will-power had overcome every obstacle to bring her into being. Ultimately, the *Great Eastern*'s story is perhaps best understood in psychological terms: she was an engineering dream, a triumph of design over function, of ambition over common sense even. Brunel was perhaps the only man in the world who could have imagined such a ship, designed her in detail and brought her into being. She was his ultimate triumph, and his greatest folly.

7

The Office, the Team and Professional Life

Brunel lived in an age and a culture where the work ethic and people's responsibilities for supporting themselves and their families were regarded as part of the moral order. Of course, there was a sharp distinction between the upper classes, most of whom lived a life of leisure, and the upper middle classes, like Brunel, who were obliged to work for a living. There was also a sharp distinction between the life of an upper-middle-class lady like Mary Brunel, holding court in her drawing room, and her husband with his obsessive devotion to work. However, the Victorians saw no contradictions here: this was the accepted social order and there is no reason to believe that Brunel ever questioned it.

Brunel lived to work, and he expected those working for him to do so as well. In a letter to one of his assistant engineers, he objected to:

> the apparent want of energy and activity on your part in attending to the Company's works . . . contrasted with an alleged devotion to amusement and amongst other things to cricket . . . I don't know why you should be less of a slave to work than I am, or Mr Brereton, or any of my assistants in town. It would rather astonish anybody if Mr Bennett should be a frequenter of Lord's cricket ground or practice billiards in the day time, and I don't know why a man having the advantages of country air and very light work should indulge them . . . You must endeavour to remove such grounds of observation.

Even by the energetic standards of his age, Brunel had an outstanding capacity for work. The office diaries for the 1840s and 1850s reveal an almost unbelievable daily schedule, with Brunel travelling, inspecting works and attending meetings from 6 or 7 in the morning until late into the evening, day after day. When did he find time to write the reams of letters and instructions, or produce his vast output of detailed design work? Another assistant, G.T. Clark, wrote the following reminiscence:

> I never met his equal for sustained power of work. After a hard day spent in preparing and delivering evidence, and after a hasty dinner, he would attend consultations till a late hour; and then, secure against interruption, sit down to his papers, and draw specifications, write letters or reports, or make calculations all through the night. If at all pressed for

time he slept in his armchair for two or three hours, and at early dawn he was ready for the work of the day. When he travelled he usually started about four or five in the morning, so as to reach his ground by daylight . . . This power of work was no doubt aided by the abstemiousness of his habits and by his light and joyous temperament. One luxury, tobacco, he indulged in to excess, and probably to his injury. At all times, even in bed, a cigar was in his mouth; and wherever he was engaged, there, near at hand, was the enormous leather cigar-case so well known to his friends, and out of which he was quite as ready to supply their wants as his own.

Did he really need to work so hard? There is no doubt that in Brunel's mind he did, in order to exercise the absolute control over his many projects that he insisted upon. This wish for control emerges time and time again in his correspondence, and was evidently something fundamental to his nature. Here he is, in 1851, on the subject of an engineer's responsibility:

The term 'Consulting Engineer' is a very vague one, and in practice has been too much used to mean a man who for a consideration sells his name, but nothing more. Now I never connect myself with an engineering work except as the Directing Engineer who, under the Directors, has the sole responsibility and control of the engineering, and is therefore 'The Engineer'; and I have always objected to the term 'Consulting Engineer'.

Naturally, in the course of Brunel's vast and varied career there were exceptions to this. He had intended to remain in total control of the building of the Great Western Railway, but when the locomotives built to his specifications went badly wrong, he was obliged to concede the management of this area to Daniel

Gooch. When the *Great Western* steamship was being built, Brunel recognised the value of others' experience, so William Patterson produced the detailed design of the hull, while Maudslay, Son & Field designed the engine. Nevertheless, these were exceptions, and this insistence on control set him apart from almost all his peers, even in this age of 'heroic engineering'. It led on occasion to some very uncomfortable situations, and the worst was the collaboration, if one can call it that, between Brunel and John Scott Russell over the building of the *Great Eastern*. Here he is, at the outset, rejecting the Eastern Steam Navigation Company's call for him to nominate a 'resident engineer' to supervise on their behalf:

> The fact is that I never embarked in any one thing to which I have so entirely devoted myself, and to which I have devoted so much time, thought, and labour, on the success of which I have staked so much reputation . . . nor was I ever engaged in a work which from its nature required for its conduct and success that it should be entrusted so entirely to my individual management and control . . . I cannot act under any supervision, or form part of any system which recognizes any adviser other than myself, or any other source of information than mine . . . nor could I continue to act if it could be assumed for a moment that the work required me to be looked after by a Director, or anybody but myself or those employed directly by me, and for me personally for that purpose. If any doubt ever arises on these points I must cease to be responsible and cease to act.

One would not guess, from reading this, that the man actually building the ship was Scott Russell, not Brunel. It will be clear, even from the few quotations given above, that Brunel was not an easy man to work for. For all his insistence on control, he could never have achieved all that he did without the substantial staff of skilled engineers, draughtsmen and clerks who worked for him. For the most part they seem to have regarded him with reverence and loyalty, but they were his servants and were there to do his bidding. They were not collaborators in the true sense of the word, and this was not really a design team. The evidence of the sketchbooks, the calculation books and the letter books suggests that almost all the original design work originated from the mind and the pen of the chief.

Brunel had never had staff working for him until he was appointed as the GWR's engineer. Even then he seems to have carried out the initial survey in a rather ad hoc way, employing a number of local surveyors on a freelance basis. In the summer of 1835 he set up office at Parliament Street, moving that December to Duke Street. He employed a chief clerk, Joseph Bennett, who was the linchpin of the office and remained with Brunel until his death. Then, very quickly, he set up a staff of engineering assistants to work on the detailed design of the line and supervise its construction. G.E. Frere, G.T. Clark and T.E. March were the Resident Engineers for the western half of the line; R.P. Brereton, J. Hammond and T.A. Bertram for the eastern half; and William Glennie for the Box Tunnel. Below them, there were several more assistant engineers, whose numbers are harder to assess. The total number of Brunel's office staff is uncertain, but Professor Buchanan has found a very helpful document, dated March 1850, a kind of circular letter which Brunel sent to his staff inviting them to send in entries for some kind of engineering design competition, which lists 33 names, about half of which are known from other documents.

Going for a job interview at Duke Street must have been an intimidating experience for any young engineer. Here is Brunel, writing on 16 January 1836 to W.G. Owen, setting out his terms:

In consequence of Mr Bennett's strong recommendation, I authorised him to write to you on the subject of your being employed on the Great Western Railway . . . but as I have not the means of judging your capability I must explain to you the terms on which you, or any gentleman, must enter the service of the Great Western Railway. The sub-assistants must be considered as working entirely for promotion, their salaries and their continued employment depend entirely on the degree of industry and ability I find they possess. Their salaries commence at £150 p.a., and may be increased progressively up to £250 and perhaps in some cases to £350 p.a. They must reside on such part of the line as required, consider their whole time, to any extent required, at the service of the Company, and will be liable to instant dismissal should they appear to me to be inefficient from any cause whatsoever and, more particularly, to consider themselves as on trial only. If these conditions appear to you encouraging you will come to Town immediately and call at my office, 18 Duke Street, Westminster.

The use of the word 'encouraging' would seem to be an instance of Brunel's mordant sense of humour. Even so, Owen evidently was encouraged, for he was taken on: eventually, in 1868, he became one of Brunel's successors as chief engineer to the GWR.

Brunel was not the monster he might seem from this letter. He was a hard taskmaster, but he was a shrewd judge, and he was perfectly capable of appreciating and acknowledging good service. Perhaps the most valued of all his staff were the chief clerk, Joseph Bennett, and Robert Pearson Brereton, who became the chief engineering assistant in 1847. In 1845 Brunel had sent Brereton to Italy to supervise the survey for the Piedmont Railway, which had turned into such a frustrating brush with Italian officialdom that Brunel wrote to the minister responsible saying that:

> My assistant, a peculiarly energetic, persevering young man, writes to me declining to remain as feeling entirely disheartened at the constant interference with every detail – and at the entire absence of confidence.

Another assistant, William Bell, had been employed for several years to assist Brunel with mathematical calculations and experiments. By 1849, with work on the South Lock at Bristol running down, there was little more for him to do, and Brunel wrote the following reference:

> [Bell] has been known to me for about ten years – I have a high respect for his integrity and zeal in the service of his employers. He is a very well informed young man in his profession and particularly also in those branches requiring mathematical knowledge which are too often neglected – he has been engaged on Docks Works as well as Railway construction and if I had an opportunity I should employ him myself.

One might think that Brunel would have rewarded failure with instant dismissal, but there are instances of him showing forbearance and a highly developed sense of justice where he valued an individual, such as William Froude. Froude had left the GWR's service to nurse his invalid father, and then returned to work for Brunel as the resident engineer on the North Devon Railway. The latter wrote, with unusual candour:

> I have been compelled to the destruction of my comfort to undertake a great deal more than I can possibly attend to

with credit or satisfaction to myself – and but for your help on the North Devon I should have dropped a huge stitch in my work.

Froude made a major error in running the project, and wrote to Brunel offering to forgo his salary. This was the reply he received:

> You did your best and the utmost I can say now I am no longer afraid of annoying you is that you made a great mistake in not perceiving the danger sooner – quite a strange unaccountable mistake but from that very circumstance it is one of those which no one could impute to anything but a very singular accident . . . You must have the goodness therefore to send me your statement for your salary.

Froude went on to a brilliant career in naval architecture and is the principal founder of modern thinking about hull design: after Brunel's death, Froude was one of the group of friends who looked after his younger son Henry Marc.

For those judged to be incompetent, though, harsher language was used. This letter was sent to a young sub-assistant called Harrison, working on the Wharncliffe Viaduct:

> My Dear Sir,
>
> I am very sorry to be under the necessity of informing you that I do not consider you to discharge efficiently the duties of assistant engineer and consequently, as I informed you yesterday, your appointment is rescinded from this day. A great want of industry is that of which I principally complain, and thus it is entirely within your power to redeem this situation . . .

Brunel went on to offer him a continued trial on the Bristol end of the line, but by an unhappy coincidence, on the same day Harrison sent him the bill for a circumferentor (an early theodolite), which Brunel had ordered him to buy. Harrison misunderstood the instruction, thinking Brunel wanted it for the Company. Brunel reopened his letter, and added:

> You have acted with reference to this in a manner I do not choose to pass over. It indicates a temper of mind which excludes all hope of your profiting from the new trial I had proposed. You will please consider yourself dismissed from the Company's service on receipt of this letter.

Brunel had another assistant in the 1830s, called S.C. Fripp. In his case Brunel, for some reason, did not resort to summary dismissal, and instead penned one of his most celebrated letters:

> Fripp. Plain gentlemanly language seems to have no effect on you. I must try stronger language and stronger methods. You are a cursed, lazy, inattentive, apathetic vagabond and if you continue to neglect my instructions I shall send you about your business. I have frequently told you, amongst other absurd, untidy habits, that of making drawings on the backs of others is inconvenient. By your cursed neglect of that you have wasted more of my time than your whole life is worth . . .

This was followed by a further, equally strong letter. One of the rich Bristol families who supported the GWR and were represented on its board was called Fripp, and this may explain why, in this case, Brunel had to be content with abuse rather than a sacking.

Behind his sometimes harsh exterior, Brunel had a strong

sense of his responsibilities as an employer. This is vividly
conveyed in a letter of 31 August 1848, when the railway boom
had crashed to a halt:

> I have generally anxieties and vexations of my own, and at
> present they are certainly not *below* the average but they are
> completely absorbed and overpowered by the pain I have to
> undergo for others. For some weeks passed, my spirits are
> completely floored by a sense of the amount of
> disappointment, annoyance and – in too many cases – deep
> distress inflicted by me, though I am but an instrument, in
> dismissing young men who have been looking forward to
> a prosperous career in their profession, unsuspicious of the
> coming storm which I, and others mixing in the world, have
> foreseen. It is *positively shocking* to see how many of these
> young engineers have looked upon their positions as
> a certainty, have been marrying, and making themselves
> happy, and now suddenly find themselves in debt and
> pennyless. You can hardly imagine what I have to undergo in
> receiving letters of entreaty which I have no power to attend
> to. Everywhere we are reducing . . .

Brunel's way with his staff might be described as an
authoritarian paternalism. His manner with contractors was
altogether more blunt, even though he depended on them.
Large-scale contracting called for remarkable organisational
skills, as Brunel found when he was obliged to run the
construction of the *Great Eastern* directly after John Scott
Russell's bankruptcy: managing over 1,000 employees was a
very different matter from running an office of about 30. Up till
that point, though, Brunel's letters show little or no
appreciation of this. He became notorious for his insistence on
unusually high standards, for imposing the strictest possible

interpretation of his contracts, and for withholding payments from the contractors for the smallest infractions. Railway works were vast and often messy, and most other engineers were prepared to accept some give-and-take on the inessentials in order to get the job done. Not so Brunel. A letter of 22 June 1836 to Messrs Grissell & Peto concerning the Wharncliffe Viaduct at Hanwell, the place where work on the GWR began, gives a good idea of the general tone:

> Gentlemen – just returned from Hanwell – observed that by far the largest proportion of the bricks upon the ground and actually in use were of a quality quite inadmissible . . . I examined the bricks on Monday last and gave particular orders to your foreman Lawrence respecting which order I find he has neglected . . . I must request that he be immediately dismissed.

As Brunel's habits became known, the contractors learnt to put their prices up when dealing with him, and on occasion it was difficult to let the contracts at all. In Brunel's defence, he saw himself as being absolutely responsible to the directors and shareholders for the way their money was being spent. This would certainly seem to have been the case when he visited the premises of the mechanical engineers Stothert & Slaughter, and saw a cracked cylinder fitted to a locomotive being made for the GWR. Their directors promptly received this broadside:

> . . . the flaw was so large that it could not escape the attention of the most careless observer . . . I do not believe that a workman would have thought of using it in the most contemptible, worst mannered shop in England – except with fraudulent intention – yet I find such a thing in that which you profess to put perfection of workmanship and materials

and upon the success of which the reputation of your house
depends . . . your workmen are spoilt, they have learned that
they may scamp their work. All confidence on my part is
completely destroyed and I should neglect my duty to the
Company if I did not now withdraw the order.

Brunel seems to have treated most of his contractors for most of
the time with an air of haughty distance. At times, though, his
relations with them became a lot worse. Among the main causes
were his habit of varying the terms and conditions of a contract
without considering himself obliged to pay extra, and the
frankly bizarre practice whereby, in the event of a dispute
between the railway company and the contractor, the arbitrator
was none other than − Brunel! The first major victim was
William Ranger, who took contract 8L for the huge cutting at
Sonning, and a number of contracts at the Bristol end of the
line. Ranger was obliged to put up a series of £5,000 bonds for
each contract, and the weather in 1836–7 was foul, slowing the
work down. Brunel seems to have added to his difficulties by
withholding payments on one ground or another, and in 1838
Ranger became insolvent.

Several other contracts at the London end had been let to
Hugh and David McIntosh, father and son. They were
experienced and well-resourced contractors, whom Brunel
ought to have valued very highly. In 1838, with some effort, he
persuaded them to take on William Ranger's contracts. Between
then and 1840 the McIntoshes experienced Brunel at his
absolute worst. He imposed his own intepretations on the
wording in the contracts, always to the contractors' detriment.
So for instance, 'coursed rubble' masonry turned out to mean
what anyone else would have called well-cut ashlar. He failed to
ensure that property was made available to them in time,
though they incurred losses as a result. He insisted that, in

place of a subsiding embankment, they build additional arches, and declined to pay extra for them. He withheld payments time and time again, on a variety of pretexts. The McIntoshes had sunk so much money in their work for the GWR that it was too late for them to cut their losses and back out: effectively Brunel was getting them to build the line and finance a good part of it with their own credit. By 1840, the withheld payments had reached £100,000. Old Hugh McIntosh died, but his son and his executors had had enough. They sued. The GWR spun the case out, and it dragged on through Britain's antiquated legal system for 20 years. In 1865 the House of Lords found for the McIntosh estate and awarded them £100,000, with twenty years' accrued interest and all costs. The McIntosh case was about the most disreputable episode in Brunel's whole career, with one possible exception.

This concerned the excavation of the Mickleton Tunnel, on the Oxford, Worcester & Wolverhampton Railway. In 1846 the contract was taken by Robert Mudge-Marchant, who was Brunel's cousin and had briefly worked for him as an assistant engineer, in partnership with a Mr Williams. By June 1851 Brunel had withheld payments from them to the tune of £34,000 for one reason and another, and they stopped work. The OWWR directors, on the other hand, thought that Mudge-Marchant and Williams owed them £6,300, and ordered Brunel to seize equipment to this value. Mudge-Marchant and Williams lined up hundreds of their navvies to defend the tunnel and their equipment. Brunel, outraged at this challenge to his authority, also assembled several hundred navvies from elsewhere on the line, and led them in an attempt to eject the Mudge-Marchant/Williams forces. Something like 3,000 navvies lined up on the two sides and it is not surprising that violence broke out. The Chipping Campden magistrates were obliged to intervene and read the Riot Act, twice. Brunel was lectured by them on his duties as a subject, and duly enrolled as a special constable to keep public order! Anyone less eminent would probably have been charged with conspiracy to cause a breach of the peace. Poor Robert Mudge-Marchant capitulated and relinquished possession of the tunnel, and in November 1851 was declared bankrupt.

Large-scale contracting in the Victorian age was a risky business, and one of the most striking points about it is how many of the contractors came to grief. Of the ones who figure in Brunel's story, William Ranger and James and Thomas Bedborough became insolvent, and Robert Mudge-Marchant was declared bankrupt. John Scott Russell's business was bankrupted by the *Great Eastern*, and C.J. Mare was bankrupted during the construction of the Saltash Bridge, though they both recovered. Of the others, Fox, Henderson & Company went bankrupt in 1858 because of problems that arose during the construction of a Danish railway, F.R. Conder went bankrupt because the bond he had deposited was stolen by the corrupt government of Naples, and in 1866 the great Samuel Morton Peto, formerly of Grissell & Peto, was ruined in the Overend & Gurney bank crash. The contractors took the biggest risks of anyone in bringing Brunel's visions into being. Without them he would have built nothing, and they deserve a generous measure of respect in any account of his work.

Railway building in Victorian Britain represented raw capitalism, red in tooth and claw. Brunel was absolutely devoted to the principles of laissez-faire economics, and vehemently opposed to any kind of state intervention in the economy. When Stephenson's Dee Bridge collapsed in 1847, with the loss of six lives, Brunel gave evidence to the official commission of inquiry, but deplored the idea of any regulation being the result:

. . . it is to be presumed that they will . . . lay down rules to be hereafter observed, in the construction of bridges. In other words, embarrass and shackle the progress of improvements of tomorrow by recording and registering as law the prejudices and errors of today.

In the 1840s and 1850s, before Gladstone's reforms of the civil service and the armed forces, these organisations were not noted for their efficiency or their capacity for reform. The Admiralty was an area of outstanding intellectual torpor, and Brunel's brushes with them over warship design and the introduction of screw propellers to ships can only have reinforced his prejudices against government bureaucracy. During the Crimean War, Brunel envisaged and designed 'gunboats' or floating batteries: largely submerged hulls which could carry siege guns with which to attack Russian ports. He presented his designs to the Admiralty in 1854 and again in 1855, but nothing happened. Brunel had received much support and encouragement in this scheme from a retired officer, General Sir John Fox Burgoyne, and in 1855 he sent the General the following letter, reporting on progress:

You assume that something has been done or is doing in the matter which I spoke to you about last month – did you not know that it had been brought within the withering influence of the Admiralty and that (of course) therefore, the curtain had dropped upon it and nothing had resulted? It would exercise the intellects of our acutest philosophers to investigate and discover what is the powerful agent which acts upon all matters brought within the range of the mere atmosphere of that department. They have an extraordinary supply of cold water and capacious and heavy extinguishers, but I was prepared for and proof against such coarse offensive measures. But they have an *unlimited* supply of some negative principle which seems to absorb and eliminate everything that approaches them . . . It is a curious and puzzling phenomenon, but in my experience it has always attended every contact with the Admiralty.

Very little of Brunel's vast output was carried out for the Crown, but during the Crimean War he did carry out one interesting project for the War Office. This came about through his friend and brother-in-law Benjamin Hawes, who was the Permanent Secretary there. The war exposed the scandalous incompetence of Britain's military organisation at almost every level, but the most shocking aspect was the spread of disease among the troops, the total failure of the army's medical arrangements, and the thousands of avoidable deaths that ensued: 34,000 soldiers out of 56,000 in the Crimea died of disease and wounds in the course of six months in 1854–5. Florence Nightingale, who campaigned fearlessly to expose the scandal and do something about it, regarded Hawes as the worst offender and her worst enemy. Yet on 16 February 1855 Hawes contacted Brunel, and asked if he could help with the design of a temporary, prefabricated hospital. Brunel took time off from the *Great Eastern*, and by 5 March he was ready to present his plans at the War Office. He had conceived designs for prefabricated timber buildings, every element of which was light enough to be carried by one or two men. Long wards, well drained and ventilated, were to be arranged opening off a long corridor, and the whole layout could be extended if need be. The buildings could be assembled by an unskilled workforce on more or less any flattish site.

Meanwhile Brunel had sent a message by telegraph to one of his assistants, John Brunton, who was working on a branch line in Dorset, simply requesting him to come to Duke Street at 6 a.m. the following morning. Brunton duly attended, and was shown in by the footman to Brunel's office where his chief, without so much as looking up, handed him a letter addressed to Hawes and ordered him to take it to the War Office at 10. Brunton had the wit and strength of mind to realise what the job would involve and demanded a rank with real authority. In late March he set sail for Turkey with the rank of major and 30 men from the Army Works Corps, and found a site for the hospital at Renkioi on the Dardanelles. Brunel, orchestrating matters in Britain, had the first shipment of components ready by the end of April and the first consignment was landed on 7 May: his instructions to Brunton were masterpieces of clarity and organisation. Two months later, 300 beds were ready, and by Christmas 1855 the whole hospital was built and all 1,000 beds were occupied. In its short existence the hospital at Renkioi treated over 1,300 patients, of whom just 50 died, a fatality rate of only 4 per cent, as compared to a fatality rate of 42 per cent in the vast barrack hospital of Scutari. It had been a remarkable example of Brunel's powers in seeing what was needed, producing exactly the right design and organising it from first conception to actual construction, including shipping, in less than six months.

By the 1850s Brunel was certainly an eminent man, his name well known to the newspaper-reading public, but he was far too busy to play much part in public or political life: he never considered standing for Parliament and serving as an MP, as both Joseph Locke and Robert Stephenson did. There was one very important public event that Brunel did make a major contribution to, and that was the Great Exhibition of 1851. Brunel helped organise and judge some of the awards in the engineering sections of the Exhibition, but his most important role was as a member of its Building Committee.

The Exhibition arose out of a series of smaller exhibitions of manufactured goods, which had been sponsored by the Royal

Society of Arts. This event, though, was envisaged as being something on an altogether larger scale, that would demonstrate the strength of Britain's industrial culture and advertise the incredible range of its manufactures to the world. Through the first half of 1850, the Building Committee were puzzling over the problem of how to construct a temporary building in Hyde Park that could be big enough to house the vast event that was envisaged, and could be ready by May 1851. A competition attracted 248 entries, but none of them seemed to be feasible, and so the Committee, led by Brunel and Robert Stephenson, produced their own design. It was for a kind of immensely long shed with brick walls and a triple-span roof, and a huge iron-and-glass dome over the centre. The dome was Brunel's particular contribution, but the design aroused great hostility for its ugliness, apparent permanence and cost, and the future of the Exhibition seemed to be in doubt.

At this point Joseph Paxton, the self-taught genius who was gardener and engineer to the Duke of Devonshire, produced his sketch for a giant glasshouse, based on those that he had built at Chatsworth. Paxton met Robert Stephenson, who was encouraging, but the key to the success of his design was his collaboration with Charles Fox, of the engineering contractors Fox, Henderson & Company. This remarkable company had developed great expertise in making large prefabricated wrought-iron buildings for various clients including the Royal Dockyards and the GWR. The Exhibition, though, demanded something on an altogether larger scale, and Paxton's design for the Crystal Palace, as it became known, at 1,848 feet long and 456 feet wide, was probably the largest single enclosed space in the world. Nevertheless, amazingly, the designs were ready by the end of July, and Fox, Henderson offered to build it for £89,950. They did so, in five months flat, and the Exhibition opened, as planned, on 1 May. It was one of the most remarkable feats of technology and organisation in the whole history of building, and Brunel had been involved in the whole extraordinary saga. He and his family were at the opening ceremony, and visited the Exhibition repeatedly in the eight months that it was open.

In 1850 it was becoming clear to the GWR that their temporary station at Paddington was no longer adequate for their fast-rising traffic, and as Brunel began to envisage its replacement, the Crystal Palace was very much in his mind. He was imagining wide iron-and-glass roofs, but he had never actually built such a thing. Events moved with the swift decisiveness characteristic of Brunel and of Victorian industry at its most impressive: on 20 December 1850 the board took the decision to go ahead with a new station; in the last week of 1850 Brunel developed the plan of Paddington as it was built on three consecutive pages of a sketchbook; on 2 January 1851 he presented outline plans to the board; and on 23 January he presented detailed plans for the first phase, with a schedule of prices from Fox, Henderson & Company. They were still finishing the Crystal Palace in Hyde Park, and Brunel had resolved that they should build his new station too. He also engaged the architect Matthew Digby Wyatt, secretary to the Building Committee, to help with the 'ornamental details', to which Brunel himself attached great importance: this was to be a cathedral of a station, of a grandeur and beauty appropriate to its status. Brunel and Wyatt also engaged Owen Jones, design guru of the age, who designed the colour scheme for the Crystal Palace, to produce a colour scheme for Paddington, but this was vetoed by the GWR's parsimonious directors.

Paddington was a rare instance of Brunel ceding his usual control over the entire design process: he sketched the whole plan and design in outline, but Fox, Henderson designed it in detail, manufactured and built it, while Wyatt worked Brunel's sketches for the decoration up into proper designs. The wrought-iron sections, like those of the Crystal Palace, were made in Fox, Henderson's works at Smethwick, and shipped by canal down to London. The great triple roof was to be covered with 'Paxton Glazing', the system of timber-framed glazing that Joseph Paxton had designed for the Chatsworth glasshouses and subsequently used for the Crystal Palace. Brunel had probably hoped that Fox, Henderson & Company would build his station at something approaching the speed they had reached for the Exhibition, but the firm were taking on too much work and becoming overstretched. It wasn't until 1855, and after many threats and imprecations, that the great train-shed was complete. Brunel also planned the vast complexes of buildings beyond for the Goods Depot, the Carriage Department and the Locomotive Department. The Great Western Hotel at the front of the station, looking onto Praed Street, was given as a separate commission to Philip Charles Hardwick, as Brunel was probably too busy to design this as well.

One of the reasons that Fox, Henderson & Company were becoming overstretched was that after the Great Exhibition closed at the end of 1851, they set to work dismantling the building and reconstructing it at Sydenham in South London, surrounded by a splendid new park, in the area which indeed became known as Crystal Palace. A 'Crystal Palace Company' had been set up, with John Scott Russell and Joseph Paxton among its directors, to reconstruct the exhibition building to a modified design, surrounded by magnificent gardens, as Victorian Britain's greatest pleasure dome or theme park. The grounds were to have big fountains, the fountains needed a good head of water, and this produced a requirement for water towers. The company's engineer, Charles Hurd Wild, produced a design for some rather slender-looking towers, and Paxton consulted Brunel. There was a considerable engineering problem here, to do with constructing a water tank which, when full, would weigh 500 tons (later raised to 1,500 tons), 200 feet in the air. Brunel started with a gentle critique of Wild's design but ended up by replacing him, and Fox, Henderson & Company built his more robust but still elegant-looking towers in 1854–6.

The Crystal Palace was destroyed by fire in 1936. Brunel's towers survived the inferno only to be demolished in 1940–41 as it was thought that they would present too recognisable a landmark for German aircraft attacking London. Paddington Station, though, remains in good order: it is one of Britain's busiest termini, but it is also one of the most historically resonant buildings of its age. It was the child of the Crystal Palace, and it is the most important physical legacy we have from that extraordinary moment in British history, which represented the zenith of Victorian culture, and of Brunel's career. Paddington is also the gateway to the Great Western Railway, to Brunel's railway empire. If one had to pick a single place to represent his achievements it might well be Paddington, but of course he has left us much more than that.

8

The Legacy

Isambard Kingdom Brunel died at his home in Duke Street on 15 September 1859. That afternoon he called his family around him and spoke to them all, and at half past ten in the evening he slipped away, peacefully and without pain. He was 53 years and 5 months old. He was buried at Kensal Green Cemetery in West London on 20 September 1859, attended by a large crowd of family, friends and colleagues. His friends knew that he had been overstraining himself for many years and he had disregarded numerous warnings; his death aroused great and widespread grief.

Perhaps the most moving tribute at the time of Brunel's death came from his friend and colleague Daniel Gooch, who wrote:

> By his death the greatest of England's engineers was lost, the man of the greatest originality of thought and power of execution, bold in his plans but right. The commercial world thought him extravagant, but although he was so, great things are not done by those who sit down and count the cost of every thought and act. He was a true and sincere friend, a man of the highest honour, and his loss was deplored by all who had the pleasure to know him.

Brunel's long-standing friend and rival Robert Stephenson died less than a month later, on 12 October. Both losses were widely reported in the newspapers as a heavy blow for engineering, and for Britain.

Before long several plans for memorials were being mooted. Brunel's family secured permission from the Dean of Westminster to install a memorial window in the Abbey, with figures of the virtues Justice, Fortitude, Faith and Charity, designed by the architect Richard Norman Shaw. A group of his engineering friends assembled to raise subscriptions for a memorial statue, but this took a good deal longer to arrange. A nine-foot bronze figure was sculpted by Carlo, Baron Marochetti, and originally destined for Parliament Square, close by Duke Street and the Institution of Civil Engineers: it was eventually erected on the Embankment, near Temple station, where it remains. The directors of the Cornwall Railway, having recently (in May 1859) opened Brunel's magnificent Saltash Bridge, felt moved to have the words 'I.K. BRUNEL | ENGINEER | 1859' placed over both of its portals.

However, engineers being the energetic, constructive people they are, Brunel's friends and colleagues in the profession were not content with these rather conventional expressions of respect. Joseph Locke, the last of the great triumvirate of railway engineers, had succeeded Robert Stephenson as President of the Institution of Civil Engineers: he and a group of colleagues planned to revive the long-dormant Clifton Bridge project and complete it as a further memorial. It is striking that this group included some of the most formidable opponents of the broad gauge, such as the engineers John Hawkshaw and George Parker Bidder, and Mark Huish, secretary of the London and North Western Railway. By coincidence Hawkshaw, as the engineer to the South Eastern Railway, was planning the extension to their new station at Charing Cross, and this required him to carry out the sad task of demolishing Brunel's Hungerford Bridge to make way for the new railway bridge. The Hungerford Bridge's suspension chains were bought for the revived company.

So the new Clifton Bridge Company started with the towers on either side of the Avon gorge almost complete, the anchorage chambers dug, and the chains from the Hungerford Bridge. John Hawkshaw and William Barlow, as its engineers, produced a revised version of Brunel's design. The towers were completed with a somewhat increased taper to them and without any of Brunel's intended Egyptian ornament. The Hungerford Bridge chains would have been sufficient for a double chain on either side with hangers at 12-foot intervals: Hawkshaw and Barlow were not happy with this and had more links manufactured to make three lines of chain for either side, with hangers at 8-foot intervals. They reduced the length of the land chains, making them steeper, and thus requiring the excavation of new anchorage chambers. The deck design, too, was changed. Brunel had envisaged a deck mainly of timber: Hawkshaw and Barlow designed a wrought-iron frame for the deck, and increased its width slightly.

It will be apparent from this summary that the Clifton Bridge as built is quite a long way from Brunel's original design. Hawkshaw and Barlow presented their revised design at the 1862 Exhibition, but unfortunately they managed to offend Brunel's family in the process, who believed that their father's role had been underplayed. The bridge was opened with great ceremony on 8 December 1864, 33 years after Brunel won the second competition (and 111 years since William Vick had died leaving his original £1,000 legacy), but sadly the Brunel family did not attend. The bridge was and is, nevertheless, a magnificent thing, as beautiful as it is useful, and it must be one of the finest memorials that any individual has ever received.

Brunel left about £89,000, enough to keep his family in comfort, but not in great wealth. He had made a habit of always investing in his own projects: most of them had been profitable, and he had made far more money from shareholdings than from his salaries and engineering fees. Had he died six years previously, before venturing a large part of his capital on the *Great Eastern*, he would surely have been worth a lot more: among his contemporaries, Robert Stephenson left about £400,000, while Joseph Locke left about £320,000. There was now no hope that the family would ever build the country house at Watcombe that Brunel had dreamed of and sketched, and before long the property there was sold.

Mary Brunel lived at 17–18 Duke Street until her death in 1881. Of their children, Isambard Junior was then 22, studying law: he became an ecclesiastical lawyer and Chancellor of the Diocese of Ely. Isambard Junior is most remembered for his biography of his father, published in 1870, on which his younger brother Henry Marc collaborated. Henry was 16 and a schoolboy at Harrow at the time of his father's death. He had shown far more of an interest in engineering, and after school he attended technical lectures at King's College, London. A number of his father's friends seem to have taken on a degree of avuncular responsibility for him, including the ship designer William Froude and the great industrialist Sir William Armstrong; in 1861 Henry entered an engineering apprenticeship with Sir William Armstrong & Company, at Elswick on the Tyne, apparently on a rather privileged basis. Henry's going to work for Armstrong may have led to a further family connection, for in 1864 his elder brother Isambard married Georgina Noble, sister of Sir William's managing director, Captain (later Sir) Andrew Noble. Later, Henry worked for the great railway engineer Sir John Hawkshaw, and in the 1860s he seems to have spent a good deal of time assisting his elder brother in the preparation of the biography that was their tribute to their father.

While Mary Brunel continued to live upstairs at Duke Street, Brunel's office on the ground floor was run for some years after his death by his principal assistant, Robert Pearson Brereton. It was Brereton who had supervised the completion of the Saltash Bridge, and from 1859 to 1864 he was building the Falmouth branch of the Cornwall Railway, with its eight timber viaducts, including the one at Collegewood which was the last to go in 1934.

In the 1870s, Henry Marc was living comfortably but unambitiously on work picked up from his father's friends, and often to be seen at the theatre (one wonders what his father would have thought!). At some point, he purchased the lease of Duke Street with the engineer John Wolfe Barry, son of Sir Charles Barry, architect of the new Palace of Westminster, and in 1878 he became Wolfe Barry's junior partner. In this capacity his most important achievement was as the structural engineer for Tower Bridge (1886–94): Wolfe Barry is always cited as the engineer for the bridge, but he himself acknowledged the crucial role that Henry played in designing its massive steel frame. Henry was certainly not cast in the same heroic mould as his father, but he was evidently an engineering designer of some distinction.

John Wolfe Barry purchased the Duke Street house, probably after Mary Brunel's death in 1881: he moved in, and the Brunels had to move out. Isambard Junior died in 1902, and Henry (who had never married) in 1903: neither of them left any children. Their sister Florence had died in 1876, aged about 28. She had been married to an Eton schoolmaster, Arthur James, and they had one daughter, Celia. In 1891 Celia Brunel James married Sir Saxton Noble, second son of Sir Andrew Noble, and Brunel's living relatives are all descended from this marriage.

Brunel's birthplace at Britain Steet in Portsmouth was demolished in the 1960s. However, the house in Lindsey Row on Cheyne Walk where he spent much of his childhood still stands. In the 1950s the row was refaced by the London County Council in an attempt to restore the original appearance of the late 17th-century Lindsey House, so the exterior looks different, but it is nevertheless the same house and it bears a Blue Plaque commemorating both Marc and Isambard. The Horsley family home at 1 High Row, Kensington still stands, as 128 Kensington Church Street: it is marked by a Blue Plaque to the previous occupant, the composer Muzio Clementi. The house remains much the same, with the drawing room where Brunel wooed Mary and took part in her family's entertainments and the studio where John Horsley painted his portraits.

Both 53 Parliament Street and 17–18 Duke Street were demolished early in the 20th century, together with a whole quarter of Georgian terraced houses, to make way for the present Treasury building. Sir John Wolfe Barry was still living in the house at Duke Street when the London County Council got around to thinking about erecting a Blue Plaque to Brunel there in 1905: he had, regretfully, to tell them that the house was under sentence of death and it came down in 1910. No record was made of the building where Brunel had lived and worked for almost half his life, but its site is readily detectable, for it was the end house, next to the Clive Steps: Brunel's ground-floor office at number 17 must have been almost exactly on the site of the present public entrance to the Cabinet War Rooms.

Brunel had left a huge archive of documents. After his death, his family gave about fifty volumes to the GWR, which had them specially bound: they passed, with the rest of the company's papers (or what remains of them) to the National Archives at Kew. A lot of the volumes are simply Brunel's copies of printed papers, but this collection also includes several letter books, and six precious volumes of 'Facts', representing his private research notes. The GWR had retained many other original Brunel documents, mostly letters and reports to the company, and these too remain in the National Archive. However, the huge quantities of engineering plans and drawings produced under Brunel's supervision at Duke Street, many of which might be regarded as works of art, all remained in the GWR's plan room at Paddington and were subsequently transferred to British Rail. No sustained attempt was ever made to separate out the historic material from the current working drawings in British Rail's plan rooms (though a good deal may have been disposed of), with the result that most of the original Brunel designs which survive are still held by Network Rail. Much of this immense collection remains unexplored, though a few of the drawings are reproduced in this book.

Many of Sir Marc's documents were given to the Institution of Civil Engineers, where they remain. The greater part of Isambard's documents, however, remained with the family,

passing eventually to Celia, Lady Noble. They were still kept by
the Noble family at Walwick Hall in Northumberland when Tom
Rolt set out to write his classic biography of Brunel in the
1950s. Since then most of this great collection has been acquired
by Bristol University Library, which remains the key source and
archive, having all of Brunel's sketchbooks, the office diaries, his
calculation books, most of his surviving correspondence and
much else besides. Taking all this material together Brunel is
probably the best-documented engineer, and he must indeed be
one of the most well-documented individuals, in British history,
even though he never published anything of significance during
his lifetime.

For most people, though, Brunel's real legacy is the series of
vast engineering works created during his lifetime of frenetic,
obsessive work. A great deal of it remains, though it should be
borne in mind that there isn't, and never has been, any catalogue
of his work. Indeed, given how over-extended Brunel was in the
1840s and 1850s, and how much of the work was being done by
his office, there would be some question as to how one could
compile such a catalogue and what one would include.

The later history of the Thames Tunnel, where his career
began and his father's career ended, has a sadly bathetic quality.
It never made a commercial return as a foot tunnel and in 1865
it was bought by the East London Railway Company, who dug
tunnels leading up to it at either end and ran an underground
railway through it. Today, this is the Rotherhithe to Wapping
section of the East London line, and travellers on the
Underground can see the arches and blocking-course which form
part of Marc's design. A few years ago, the tunnel was given a
dry-lining of concrete, though it was saved from more drastic
alteration by a major campaign led by the Victorian Society and
the Newcomen Society. The tunnel cannot normally be seen by
the public, but at its south end in Rotherhithe the engine house

has been converted by a charitable trust into a museum of the Thames Tunnel.

Brunel's greatest legacy is as a railway builder: he designed or supervised the design and construction of over 1,200 miles of railway in England and Wales, most of which remains in use, forming a substantial proportion of our modern network. The GWR remained true to his name and to the seven-foot gauge for a long time after his death. Many people in the company must have known that the broad gauge would come to an end some time, certainly after the GWR bought the West Midlands company in 1861, which brought a large mileage of standard-gauge line into its network, obliging them to lay mixed-gauge lines in order to run both kinds of trains. The greatest champion of the broad gauge, Daniel Gooch, returned to the GWR as its Chairman in 1865. During the 1870s and 1880s the company was converting the outlying stretches of its network and running more and more 4' 8½" gauge trains, but so far as Gooch was concerned abolishing the broad gauge really was a case of 'over my dead body', and it could not be contemplated until after his death in 1889. However, the costs associated with laying mixed-gauge tracks and running both kinds of train were a heavy burden, and at last the evil moment could not be put off any longer. On 20 May 1892 the last broad-gauge express train left Paddington for Penzance. Over a weekend, the whole of the remaining 171 miles of mixed-gauge track were converted to the 4' 8½" gauge. It was the end of a great engineering vision, and one which, had Brunel got his crucial opportunity just a few years earlier, might well have grasped and defined the future.

Even with the loss of the broad gauge, Brunel's railways remain an astonishing achievement. His London to Bristol line, above all, has always been acknowledged as one of the masterpieces of railway design. Having been conceived at the generous scale needed to accommodate the broad gauge, it hasn't needed nearly so much widening and alteration as other main lines, and its grand and scenic qualities are remarkably well preserved. Other railway lines run through beautiful countryside, but surely no other line was designed and adorned with such conscious and lavish care as this one. The run from Bristol to Bath in particular, through the succession of castellated tunnels, alongside the Avon in its green valley, over the battlemented Bath Viaduct, through the Elizabethan station, through the balustraded cutting of Sydney Gardens and up to the magnificent portal of the Box Tunnel, must be the most splendid architectural experience available anywhere on Britain's railway network. For this reason, as well as for all the historical reasons, the London to Bristol main line is currently an official candidate for the status of World Heritage Site.

Several of Brunel's stations remain, though in varying states of preservation. The terminus at Bristol Temple Meads survives complete, though the station was greatly extended in the 1870s. Brunel's original shed eventually fell out of use for railway purposes, leaving the later buildings to serve as the present station. For many years, his great timber-roofed train-shed had to endure the indignity of housing a car park, though it has recently been splendidly refurbished, and now houses the Empire and Commonwealth Museum. The grand Elizabethan station at Bath remains in railway use and in good condition, though it lost its timber roof at a very early stage.

At Swindon, Brunel's railway village survives almost complete. The GWR's vast 'engineering establishment', however, grew beyond all recognition, before its eventual closure in 1986. Some of the workshop buildings survive and part of them houses STEAM, the museum of the GWR, one of the main resources for those wishing to understand this major part of railway history. The great iron-and-glass roof of Paddington, happily, remains in use as one of Britain's best-loved railway stations: its thorough renovation in 1988–91 was one of British Rail's last great achievements.

The fiasco of the South Devon Atmospheric Railway is remembered as Brunel's worst failure, but the picturesque beauty of his line as it winds along the coast from Exeter to Newton Abbot and then through the gentle green countryside to Plymouth, would be a fine legacy by itself. The distinctive Italianate architecture created by Brunel can still be seen in the stations at Dawlish, Exminster and Torre, and in the engine houses at Torre and Starcross.

Many of the bridges have survived well. The Wharncliffe Viaduct and Maidenhead Bridge remain in daily use, though doubled in width in the 1870s, and continue to carry dozens of trains every day. Many of Brunel's elliptical arches still carry roads over the London to Bristol main line. Indeed, many fine masonry bridges by Brunel survive on or over our railway network: the skew bridge carrying the South Devon line over a road in Plympton (at a 63-degree skew) is one case in point; the elegant six-arch viaduct that he built in 1840 to carry the Taff Vale Railway over the Taff at Quakers' Yard in Glamorgan is another.

The timber bridges have all been replaced: Brunel only meant them to be temporary, and knew that they wouldn't last, but there are still numerous reminders of them. Some of the masonry piers of his spectacular Cornish viaducts were retained and still carry the railway lines on steel trusses in place of the original timber work, as at Liskeard, or at St Pinnock and Largin in the Glynn Valley. In a number of other places the tall masonry piers survive, abandoned like relics of some ancient civilisation, as at Moorswater in Cornwall, or at Ivybridge and Glazebrook in the south of Devon.

The iron bridges present a more mixed picture. Of the cast-iron bridges, a handful are known to survive: the under-line bridges have almost certainly all been replaced with steel or concrete for safety reasons. The Uxbridge Road Bridge, just up from the Wharncliffe Viaduct, has big 20th-century steel girders, though the grimy abutment walls and one octagonal column remain from the bridge which gave Brunel so much trouble. Just down the road from it, the Windmill Bridge remains in good order. Another cast-iron bridge close by Paddington Station, dating from 1839, was rediscovered (or recognised) in 2003, just in time to save it from demolition: it has since become clear that this is Brunel's earliest surviving iron bridge. It was saved by being dismantled, by cooperative efforts between English Heritage, Westminster City Council and British Waterways, and there are plans to reconstruct it close to its original site.

Brunel's wrought-iron bridges survive somewhat better: the great 200-foot arched truss at Windsor is still in railway service. Of the Chepstow Bridge the original cast-iron columns survive, as does the massive stone abutment on the English side, but sadly the great 300-foot span trusses had to be replaced in steel in 1962. The Balmoral Bridge continues to carry a public highway. The Saltash Bridge remains in good condition, as one of the sights of the South-West, and the only suspension bridge in service on Britain's railway network. The Crystal Palace in Sydenham burnt down in 1936, and Brunel's great water towers came down in 1940–41. The great brick bases survive and there is a museum dedicated to the history of Crystal Palace close by the western one.

It is important to remember that there is no catalogue of Brunel's works. The bridges and buildings which are referred to in books such as this one represent the tip of an iceberg. There is no doubt that many bridges and buildings by him have been largely or completely forgotten because they have been demolished: John Binding's book on the Cornish timber viaducts serves as a demonstration of this, and of how far these forgotten works can be recovered. One might add that Brunel designed so much that it is quite likely that there are many unrecognised works by him still standing.

Brunel's legacy as a ship designer is just as extraordinary in its way. He had to endure the sadness of seeing his first great ship, the *Great Western*, broken up in 1857: only her ship's bell remains, today owned by the SS Great Britain Trust. The *Great Eastern*, Brunel's 'great babe', has often been regarded as an unlucky ship. After eight honourable years of service laying cables, she was laid up at Milford Haven for another twelve. What followed was an ignominious fate: in 1885 the vast ship, still the largest in the world, was bought by one Edward de Mattos for £25,000, and then leased by David Lewis of Liverpool, founder of the city's department store, as a floating entertainment establishment and concert hall. The ship was moored in the Mersey, the decks were filled with stalls and visitors paid a shilling a head, to include the price of the ferry. At last in 1888 de Mattos sold the great ship to Henry Bath & Sons, a firm of ship breakers on the Mersey. They sold the materials for £58,000, but it took 200 men two years to break up Brunel's massive double-skinned hull, twice as long as they had anticipated: not even the ship breakers could make a profit out of the *Great Eastern*. The timber launching ways, the scene of the desperate efforts to launch her, are still visible at low water in the foreshore off Millwall on the Isle of Dogs, and a Blue Plaque has been fixed to the remaining buildings of John Scott Russell's yard, now known as Burrell's Wharf.

The *Great Britain* has also had a chequered career, but in her case it is a story with a happy ending. After several years of service as a steamship on the Australian run, she was laid up in 1875 for seven years. In 1882 she was bought by Antony Gibbs & Son, a firm owned by a Bristol family with strong links to

Brunel and the GWR. Her engines were removed, and she did a few more years' service as a sailing ship. In 1886 the *Great Britain* was sold on to the Falkland Islands Company, and consigned to use as a floating hulk or storehouse for wool, off Port Stanley. Finally, in 1936, the rusting hulk was towed to Sparrow Cove and scuttled: it seemed as if she had reached her final resting place. Since then, thanks to the heroic efforts of Ewan Corlett and others, the *Great Britain* has been rescued. In 1970 she was lifted onto a giant barge and brought home to Bristol, and vested in the care of the SS Great Britain Trust. A loving and painstaking restoration began, which still continues, and today Brunel's iron ship is one of the great sights of the city which gave him his greatest opportunities.

In the 1920s and 1930s, when Victorian culture was routinely derided or ignored, and industrial history seen as something grimy and 'Dickensian', Brunel's reputation perhaps reached its lowest ebb. His grand-daughter, Lady Noble, published her beautifully written study of the two Brunels, father and son, in 1938, and this may have sparked a revival of interest. Tom Rolt's classic biography, published in 1957, represents the start of contemporary interest in the great man: Rolt, indeed, was one of the founding figures of industrial archaeology. Rising interest since then has seen detailed studies of the three great ships, and the publication of Adrian Vaughan's 'revisionist' biography in 1991, highlighting the darker aspects of Brunel's character and career, that neither Lady Noble nor Rolt had wished to dwell on. None of this, however, could really have prepared one for the surge of interest in recent years, typified by Brunel being voted the second 'Greatest Briton' (to Churchill) by a very large audience of television viewers, in a BBC TV series in 2003. Brunel was a creative genius, a truly great man, but how can one explain the degree to which his modern reputation overshadows that of his contemporaries, even Telford and the Stephensons?

First, perhaps, one can point to the range of his achievements and abilities. In modern terms, these would cover at least eight different professional disciplines: surveyor, civil engineer, structural engineer, mechanical engineer, architect, ship designer, project manager, quantity surveyor – and Brunel excelled in all of them, most if not all of the time. He was one of the last generation before the Industrial Revolution, which he did so much to speed, matured to the point of creating a culture of specialisation. Every one of these subjects has grown, to the point where no one individual could master them all now: Brunel was the 19th century's answer to the Renaissance Man. Tom Rolt remarked that, had Brunel been born in the 16th century, he would have been one of the great artists.

Then there is his charisma, the force of personality which leaps off the page in so much of his correspondence. Brunel's striving, astringent spirit would not put up with second best, in things or individuals. Such people are not easy to live with, but as George Bernard Shaw observed, since the reasonable man adapts himself to his circumstances, all progress must depend on the unreasonable man.

In the end, Brunel was a man of his time: to see him as a modern figure is to diminish as well as misunderstand him. In his qualities, both his vices and virtues, he was decidedly un-modern. The last man in the world to listen to subordinates, jealous of his pre-eminence, a harsh manager, bullying and intractable to contractors, and seemingly careless of the safety and well-being of the thousands of humble workmen who turned his vast conceptions into reality. Contemptuous of his own safety, ultimately of his own health. Always willing to take a personal or a financial risk. Always willing to favour innovation over established methods. Always willing to use new ideas, even on very large projects with huge budgets. Usually rigorous about testing the ideas, but sometimes, simply too optimistic about them. Absolutely devoted to the principles of economic liberalism and hostile to almost any form of state interference.

Brunel is a strange hero, in some ways, for a society as timid, as obsessed by safety, as concerned for the environment, as anxious about reaching consensus, as addicted to denigrating greatness and apportioning blame, and as dominated by the state, as our own. Could our society produce another Brunel? It is difficult to see how. He was a man from another age, an age in which heroic individualism was seen as the principal motive force in human affairs, and in which men could act accordingly. A great man – the greatest engineer in history.

Chronology

1806
9 APRIL. Isambard Kingdom Brunel is born, in a terraced house in Britain Street, Portsmouth.

1807
SUMMER. The Brunel family move to 4 Lindsey Row, Chelsea.
1 MAY. The slave trade is outlawed in Britain and its colonies.

1811
George III becomes incurably deranged: his eldest son George, Prince of Wales, becomes Prince Regent.

1813
Isambard is sent to the Reverend Weedon Butler's school, Chelsea.

1815
18 JUNE. The Battle of Waterloo.

1818
Marc Brunel patents his first design for a 'tunnelling shield'.

1820
Isambard is sent to school in France, at the college at Caen, then at the Lycée Henri IV in Paris, subsequently apprenticed to the watchmaker Louis Breguet.
29 JANUARY. King George III dies at Windsor: the Prince Regent becomes king as George IV.

1821
18 MAY. Marc and Sophia Brunel are arrested for debt and sent to the King's Bench Prison, Southwark.

1822
AUGUST. Isambard returns from France and starts work in his father's office.

1823
SUMMER. Marc and Isambard start work on the development of the 'Gaz Engine' which occupies much of their time until 1833.
SEPTEMBER. Marc Brunel publishes his design for a rectangular tunnelling shield and finalises his scheme for a tunnel beneath the River Thames.

1824
FEBRUARY. The Thames Tunnel Company is established.

JUNE. Marc Brunel moves his office and his family to 30 Bridge Street, Blackfriars.

1825

2 MARCH. The first stone is laid of the Rotherhithe shaft of the Thames Tunnel.
27 SEPTEMBER. Opening of the Stockton & Darlington Railway, the world's first locomotive-drawn railway.
28 NOVEMBER. Work begins on the excavation of the Thames Tunnel.

1826

3 JANUARY. Isambard is appointed as resident engineer to the Thames Tunnel.

1827

17 MAY. The first flood of the Thames Tunnel.
7 OCTOBER. Isambard is badly injured by falling into a water tank at the Thames Tunnel works yard.

1828

11 JANUARY. The second flood of the Thames Tunnel. Isambard is seriously injured. The tunnel project goes into abeyance.

1829

NOVEMBER. Brunel sends in four entries for the competition for the Clifton Bridge, Bristol.

1830

26 JUNE. Death of King George

IV: succession of William IV.
15 SEPTEMBER. The Liverpool & Manchester Railway, the world's first purpose-built passenger railway, is opened.
15 NOVEMBER. The Duke of Wellington's government resigns, ending over 20 years of Tory administration, and is replaced by Earl Grey's Whig administration, committed to parliamentary reform.

1831

JANUARY. Brunel sends in a design for the second competition for the Clifton Bridge.
16 MARCH. Brunel's design for the Clifton Bridge is accepted.
27 AUGUST. The foundation stone of the Clifton Bridge is laid. Work starts, but then stops almost immediately.
OCTOBER. Serious riots in Bristol: Brunel enlists as a special constable.
20 NOVEMBER. Brunel is commissioned to design a new dock at Monkwearmouth, Sunderland, County Durham.
5 DECEMBER. Brunel takes his first ride on a train, on the Liverpool & Manchester Railway.

1832

7 JUNE. The first Parliamentary Reform Act becomes law.

1833

7 MARCH. Brunel is appointed as engineer to the Bristol Railway Company.

9 MARCH. Brunel sets out, with William Townshend, to survey a route for the Bristol Railway.
30 JULY. Brunel publishes his route for the Bristol Railway.
27 AUGUST. Brunel is confirmed as engineer to the Bristol Railway, which changes its name to the Great Western Railway at the same meeting.

1834

JANUARY. Brunel and his staff complete parliamentary plans for the Great Western Railway.
JULY. A Treasury loan of £270,000 to the Thames Tunnel Company is approved.
25 JULY. The Great Western Railway Company's first parliamentary bill is rejected by the House of Lords.

1835

31 AUGUST. The GWR's second parliamentary bill receives royal assent.
SEPTEMBER. Brunel is appointed engineer to the Bristol & Exeter Railway and the Cheltenham & Great Western Union Railway.
OCTOBER. Brunel presents his ideas for a seven-foot railway gauge to the GWR directors.
OCTOBER. Brunel dines with the GWR directors at Radley's Hotel, Blackfriars, and first proposes the idea of building a steamship to cross the Atlantic.
DECEMBER. Brunel acquires the lease of 18 Duke Street,

Westminster and moves in.
DECEMBER. Brunel is appointed as engineer for the Hungerford Footbridge, London.
DECEMBER. Brunel is appointed as engineer to the Merthyr & Cardiff (or Taff Vale) Railway.

1836

JANUARY. Contracts are let for the shafts of the Box Tunnel, Wiltshire.
FEBRUARY. Work starts on the GWR at the Wharncliffe Viaduct, Hanwell, West London.
MARCH. Work is resumed on the Thames Tunnel.
4 MARCH. The first public meeting of the Great Western Steamship Company.
MAY. Brunel becomes engaged to Mary Horsley.
5 JULY. Brunel is married to Mary Horsley at St Mary's, Kensington.
27 AUGUST. The second foundation-stone ceremony for the Clifton Bridge.

1837

Brunel's son Isambard Junior is born.
20 JUNE. Queen Victoria succeeds to the throne of Great Britain.
22 JULY. The steamship *Great Western* is launched at Bristol.

1838

31 MARCH. The SS *Great Western* makes its first voyage

under steam: Brunel is seriously injured following a fire in the engine room.

7 APRIL. The *Great Western* embarks on her maiden voyage.

23 APRIL. The *Great Western* arrives in New York.

31 MAY. The GWR runs its first train from Paddington to Maidenhead.

4 JUNE. The GWR opens its passenger services from Paddington to Maidenhead.

1 AUGUST. The Act to abolish slavery in the British empire (passed in 1833) comes into full legal force.

NOVEMBER. Brunel starts work on the design of a hull for a new steamship, the future SS *Great Britain*.

1839

7 JANUARY. A crucial meeting of GWR shareholders votes to retain the broad gauge, by 7,790 to 6,145.

19 JULY. The keel of the *Great Britain* is laid in Bristol.

1840

30 MARCH. The GWR opens its line as far as Reading.

31 AUGUST. The GWR opens its line from Bristol to Bath.

1841.

Brunel is appointed as engineer to the Oxford Railway.

MARCH. The Box Tunnel is completed.

24 MARCH. Marc Brunel is knighted by Queen Victoria.

30 JUNE. The GWR runs its first continuous train service from Paddington to Bristol.

1842.

Brunel's son Henry Marc is born.

JANUARY. The main construction of the Thames Tunnel is completed.

1 JULY. The Bristol & Exeter Railway opens from Bridgwater to Taunton.

1843

19 JULY. The launch of the SS *Great Britain* in the Floating Harbour, Bristol.

SUMMER. Brunel visits Italy, and is appointed engineer to the Piedmont Railway.

1844.

Brunel is appointed engineer to the Berkshire & Hampshire Railway, Monmouth & Hereford Railway, Oxford & Rugby Railway, Oxford, Worcester & Wolverhampton Railway, South Wales Railway and the Wiltshire, Somerset & Weymouth Railway.

1 MAY. The Bristol & Exeter Railway opens to Exeter.

JULY. The South Devon Railway Company obtains its Act of Parliament to build a line operated with conventional locomotives.

1845

SPRING. Work begins on the South Devon railway, now

designed to run using the
atmospheric system.

1 MAY. The Hungerford
Footbridge opens to the public.

26 JULY. The maiden voyage
of the SS *Great Britain* to New
York.

AUGUST. Brunel is appointed
engineer to the Cornwall Railway
and the West Cornwall Railway.

1846

25 JUNE. The Corn Laws are
repealed by Sir Robert Peel's
Conservative government,
ushering in an era of unrestricted
free trade: Peel's government falls
soon afterwards, as a direct result.

22 SEPTEMBER. SS *Great
Britain* runs aground in Dundrum
Bay.

DECEMBER. Brunel visits
Dundrum Bay to inspect the *Great
Britain*.

1847

Brunel's daughter, Florence Mary,
is born.

AUGUST. Brunel buys land at
Watcombe, near Torquay, Devon,
intending to build a country house
there.

AUGUST. The South Devon Railway starts running train services
using atmospheric traction from
Exeter to Teignmouth.

1848.

Brunel acquires the lease of 17,
Duke Street and links it to
number 18.

The campaign for the People's
Charter, demanding the vote for all
British men, gains momentum,
attracting over 3,000,000
signatures, causing great alarm in
government and among the upper
and middle classes. Most of the
European monarchies are
convulsed by revolution in the
course of the year.

FEBRUARY. The South Devon
Railway opens its line from Teignmouth to Newton Abbot using
atmospheric traction.

19 AUGUST. Brunel recommends
that atmospheric traction be
abandoned on the South Devon
Railway.

1849

MAY. Work commences on the
Chepstow Bridge, over the tidal
River Wye.

20 JUNE. The first tube of
Robert Stephenson's Britannia
Bridge over the Menai Straits is
floated into position, with Brunel
in attendance.

8 OCTOBER. The Windsor
Railway Bridge is opened.

12 DECEMBER. Sir Marc Brunel
dies, aged 80.

1850

Brunel is appointed to the
Building Committee for the Great
Exhibition.

JUNE. The South Wales Railway
opens from Chepstow to Landore.

DECEMBER. Brunel begins work
on the designs for Paddington
Station.

1851

1 MAY. Brunel and his family attend the opening of the Great Exhibition, Hyde Park.
31 DECEMBER. The Great Exhibition closes. The components of the Crystal Palace are bought by a new company, to be reconstructed at Sydenham, South London.

1852

MARCH. Brunel makes the first calculations and sketches for a gigantic iron ship, the origin of the idea of the *Great Eastern*.
JULY. Brunel is appointed engineer to the Eastern Steam Navigation Company.
AUGUST. West Cornwall Railway opens from Truro to Penzance.

1853

APRIL. The second span of the Chepstow Bridge is opened to traffic.
NOVEMBER. Brunel appointed to design two watertowers for the new Crystal Palace, replacing Charles Wild.
22 DECEMBER. John Scott Russell signs a contract to build Brunel's 'great ship' for the Eastern Steam Navigation Company.

1854.

Scott Russell leases the Napier Yard, adjacent to his own yard on the Isle of Dogs, and work starts on the 'great ship' later named the *Great Eastern*.

2 JANUARY. The South Wales Railway opens from Carmarthen to Haverfordwest.
16 JANUARY. The first train runs out of the departure side of the new Paddington Station.

1855

JANUARY. Sophia, Lady Brunel, dies aged 80.
16 FEBRUARY. Brunel is asked by Benjamin Hawes of the War Office to produce designs for a prefabricated hospital, to be built in Turkey for soldiers wounded in the Crimean War.
MAY. The prefabricated hospital is constructed at Renkioi on the Dardanelles, supervised by John Brunton.

1856

Work is in progress on the central column and on the two great trusses for the Saltash Bridge.
4 FEBRUARY. John Scott Russell is declared bankrupt: work on the *Great Eastern* is suspended.
23 MAY. Work is resumed on the *Great Eastern*.
19 SEPTEMBER. Scott Russell resigns, leaving Brunel in sole charge of work on the *Great Eastern*.

1857.

Brunel is working on designs for the East Bengal Railway.
AUTUMN. Brunel's road bridge at Balmoral is completed and opened.
1 SEPTEMBER. The first (Cornish) span of the Saltash

Bridge is floated into position, with Brunel supervising.

3 NOVEMBER. Abortive attempt to launch the *Great Eastern*.

NOVEMBER TO JANUARY. Repeated attempts are made to launch the *Great Eastern*.

1858

31 JANUARY. The *Great Eastern* is floated on the high tide.

SUMMER. Brunel is seriously ill, and is diagnosed as suffering from Bright's Disease (glomerulo-nephritis).

10 JULY. The second (Devon) span of the Saltash Bridge is floated into position, supervised by R. P. Brereton.

NOVEMBER. The Eastern Steam Navigation Company is dissolved, with enormous losses: the *Great Eastern* is bought by the newly formed Great Ship Company.

WINTER, 1858–9. Brunel and his family go on a long tour of Italy, the Mediterranean and Egypt.

1859

2 MAY. The Royal Albert Bridge, Saltash, is opened to traffic.

6 MAY. Brunel and his family return to England.

5 SEPTEMBER. Brunel collapses on board the SS *Great Eastern*, the day before it is due to sail.

6 SEPTEMBER. Brunel orders the sale of the Watcombe estate.

8 SEPTEMBER. An explosion on board the SS *Great Eastern*, while at sea, kills six sailors and injures many others.

15 SEPTEMBER. Brunel dies at Duke Street aged 53, with his family around him.

Bibliography

Michael R. Bailey, ed. *Robert Stephenson – The Eminent Engineer*, Ashgate
  Publishing, Aldershot, 2003.
Richard Beamish, *Memoir of the Life of Sir Marc Isambard Brunel*,
  London, 1862.
Patrick Beaver, *The Big Ship – Brunel's Great Eastern, A Pictorial History*,
  Evelyn, 1969.
John Binding, *Brunel's Cornish Viaducts*, Atlantic Transport Publishers,
  Penryn, 1993.
John Binding, *Brunel's Royal Albert Bridge*, Twelveheads Press, Truro,
  1997.
John Binding, *Brunel's Bristol Temple Meads*, Oxford Publishing, Hersham,
  2001.
Steven Brindle, *Paddington Station – Its History and Architecture*, English
  Heritage, London, 2004.
Isambard Brunel, *The Life of Isambard Kingdom Brunel, Civil Engineer*,
  Longman, Green & Co., London, 1870.
Angus Buchanan, *Brunel – The Life and Times of Isambard Kingdom Brunel*,
  Hambledon & London, London, 2002.
Paul Clements, *Marc Isambard Brunel*, Longmans, London, 1970.
F.R. Conder, *Personal Recollections of English Engineers*, Hodder &
  Stoughton, London, 1868, reprinted as *The Men Who Built Railways*,
  ed. J. Simmons, Thomas Telford Publishers, London, 1983.
Ewan Corlett, *The Iron Ship – The History and Significance of Brunel's Great
  Britain*, Moonraker Press, Bradford-on-Avon, 1975.
George S. Emmerson, *John Scott Russell, A Great Victorian Engineer and
  Naval Architect*, John Murray, London, 1977.
Andre Gren, *The Foundation of Brunel's Great Western Railway*, Silver Link
  Publishing, Kettering, 2003.
Denis Griffiths, *Brunel's Great Western*, Patrick Stephens,
  Wellingborough, 1985.
E. Kentley, A.Hudson & J. Peto, eds., *Isambard Kingdom Brunel – Recent
  Works*, The Design Museum, London, 2000.

E. T. MacDermot, *History of the Great Western Railway*, Vol. I, 1833–63,
    Great Western Railway Company, London, 1927.
Celia Brunel Noble, *The Brunels: Father and Son*, Cobden-Sanderson,
    London, 1938.
Sir Alfred Pugsley, ed., *The Works of Isambard Kingdom Brunel – An
    Engineering Appreciation*, Institution of Civil Engineers, London, 1976.
L. T. C. Rolt, *Isambard Kingdom Brunel*, Longmans Green, London, 1957,
    republished by Penguin Books, Harmondsworth, 1970.
Jack Simmons, *The Railways of Britain*, Macmillan, London, 1968.
Jack Simmons, ed., *The Birth of the Great Western Railway – Extracts from
    the Diary and Correspondence of George Henry Gibbs*, Ada

Index

Picture Credits

SECTION ONE   PAGE 1 British Museum (top), Public Record Office (bottom); PAGE 2 NRM – Pictorial Collection/Science and Society Picture Library (top), The Nobles (bottom); PAGE 3 Stephen Brunel Hurst (top and bottom); PAGE 4 Science Museum Pictorial/Science and Society Picture Library (top right), Beamish/Institution of Civil Engineers (middle), Ironbridge Gorge Museum (bottom); PAGE 5 Public Record Office (top), National Railway Museum/Science and Society Picture Library (bottom); PAGE 6 NRM – Pictorial Collection/ Science and Society Picture Library (top), National Portrait Gallery (bottom); PAGE 7 STEAM Museum of the Great Western Railway (top), National Railway Museum/Science and Society Picture Library (bottom); PAGE 8 Science Museum Pictorial/Science and Society Picture Library (top), Private Collection/Bridgeman Art Library (bottom).

SECTION TWO   PAGE 1 NRM – Pictorial Collection/Science and Society Picture Library (top and bottom); PAGES 2–3 Science Museum/Science and Society Picture Library; PAGES 4–5 NRM – Pictorial Collection/Science and Society Picture Library; PAGE 6 Public Record Office (top), Getty Images (bottom); PAGE 7 SS *Great Britain* Trust (top), National Maritime Museum (bottom); PAGE 8 Science Museum Library/Science and Society Picture Library (top), SS *Great Britain* Trust (bottom).

SECTION THREE   PAGE 1 Julia Elton (top), Getty Images (bottom); PAGES 2–3 Science Museum/Science and Society Picture Library; PAGES 4–5 Science Museum Archive/Science and Society Picture Library; PAGES 6–7 Guildhall Library, Corporation of London, UK/Bridgeman Art Library (top – and contd top page 7), Getty Images (bottom); PAGE 7 Public Record Office (bottom); PAGE 8 Illustrated London News (top), PA Pic Select (bottom).

blog and newsletter

For literary discussion, author insight,
book news, exclusive content,
recipes and giveaways, visit the
Weidenfeld & Nicolson blog and
sign up for the newsletter at:

www.wnblog.co.uk

For breaking news, reviews and exclusive competitions
Follow us @wnbooks
Find us facebook.com/WNfiction